The Soviet Army
Tactics and Organization

1949

Prepared under the direction of
The Chief of the Imperial General Staff.

THE WAR OFFICE,
April, 1949

The Naval & Military Press Ltd

Published by the
The Naval & Military Press
in association with the Royal Armouries

Unit 10 Ridgewood Industrial Park,
Uckfield, East Sussex, TN22 5QE
Tel: +44 (0) 1825 749494
Fax: +44 (0) 1825 765701

MILITARY HISTORY AT YOUR FINGERTIPS
www.naval-military-press.com

ONLINE GENEALOGY RESEARCH
www.military-genealogy.com

ONLINE MILITARY CARTOGRAPHY
www.militarymaproom.com

ROYAL ARMOURIES

The Library & Archives Department at the Royal Armouries Museum, Leeds, specialises in the history and development of armour and weapons from earliest times to the present day. Material relating to the development of artillery and modern fortifications is held at the Royal Armouries Museum, Fort Nelson.

For further information contact:
Royal Armouries Museum, Library, Armouries Drive,
Leeds, West Yorkshire LS10 1LT
Royal Armouries, Library, Fort Nelson, Down End Road, Fareham PO17 6AN

Or visit the Museum's website at
www.armouries.org.uk

In reprinting in facsimile from the original, any imperfections are inevitably reproduced and the quality may fall short of modern type and cartographic standards.

Printed and bound by CPI Antony Rowe, Eastbourne

RESTRICTED

DISTRIBUTION

(*See Catalogue of War Office Publications, Part II*)

R.A.C., R.A., R.E., R. Sigs., Inf., R.A.S.C., R.A.O.C. and R.E.M.E.
SCALE B

CONTENTS

	Page
GLOSSARY OF TERMS	iv

Section

CHAPTER 1—INTRODUCTION

1. Object of this pamphlet	1
2. General	1

CHAPTER 2—HISTORY OF THE RED ARMY

3. The Red Army, 1918–46	2
4. Characteristics of the Soviet soldier in battle	4

CHAPTER 3—COMMAND AND CONTROL

5. The High Command	5
6. Military districts	7
7. Political control in the Armed Forces	8

CHAPTER 4—POST-WAR REORGANIZATION OF THE SOVIET ARMY

8. General	10
9. Soviet Army divisions	11
10. Divisional and unit staffs	12

CHAPTER 5—TACTICS—THE OFFENSIVE

11. Major offensives	13
12. Advance to contact and encounter battle	13
13. Preparation for a major offensive	20
14. The assault	23
15. Night attack	25
16. Pursuit	26
17. Air support in the offensive	27

Section	Page

CHAPTER 6—TACTICS—DEFENCE AND WITHDRAWAL

18. General	28
19. Army defensive area	28
20. Deployment of a rifle division	30
21. Anti-tank defence	30
22. Reserves and counter-attack	32
23. Artillery support	32
24. Anti-aircraft defence	32
25. Air support in defence	33
26. Summary of defences	33
27. Tank and mechanized divisions in defence	34
28. Withdrawal	35

CHAPTER 7—TACTICS—SPECIAL CONDITIONS

29. Fighting in built-up areas	36
30. Winter warfare	37
31. River crossing	38
32. Partisan warfare	40

CHAPTER 8—AIRBORNE OPERATIONS

33. General	42
34. Preparation and operation	44
35. Air support	46

CHAPTER 9—SUPPLY IN THE FIELD

36. Administration	46

CHAPTER 10—TRAINING AND CONDITIONS OF SERVICE

37. Training	49
38. Conditions of service	50

CHAPTER 11—EQUIPMENT

39. General	52
40. Signals	54
41. Weapons	56

APPENDICES

A.	High Command	77
B.	A typical Soviet front	78
C.	A typical Soviet rifle Army	79
D.	Organization chart of a rifle division	80
E.	Organization chart of a rifle regiment	81
F.	Organization chart of a mechanized division	82
G.	Organization chart of a mechanized regiment	83
H.	Organization chart of a heavy tank self-propelled gun regiment	84
J.	Organization chart of a tank division	85
K.	Organization chart of a 'Breakthrough' artillery division and anti-aircraft division	86
L.	Personnel and equipment table for a rifle division	87
M.	Personnel and equipment table for a rifle regiment	88
N.	Personnel and equipment table for a rifle battalion	89
O.	Personnel and equipment table for a mechanized division	90
P.	Personnel and equipment table for a mechanized regiment	91
Q.	Personnel and equipment table for a tank division	92
R.	Comparison between British and Soviet units	93
S.	Headquarters of a rifle division	94
T.	Headquarters of a rifle regiment and battalion	96
U.	A rifle division in defence	facing page 98
V.	A reinforced medium tank battalion in defence	98

GLOSSARY OF TERMS

1. **Medium self-propelled gun**—A field gun mounted on a medium tank chassis.
2. **Heavy self-propelled gun**—A field or medium gun mounted on a heavy tank chassis.
3. **Front**—A Soviet formation equivalent to a British army group.
4. **A reinforced unit**—A unit with other arms under command.
5. **Fire sack**—A pocket surrounded on three sides by anti-tank weapons, into which it is hoped to entice enemy tanks, and there destroy them.
6. **JS tank**—A Joseph Stalin type heavy tank.
7. **AAMG**—Anti-aircraft machine gun.
8. **SMG**—Sub-machine gun.
9. **Partisan**—A member of light irregular troops employed in special enterprises, usually operating and based in enemy occupied territory.
10. **RL**—Rocket launcher.

RESTRICTED

CHAPTER 1

INTRODUCTION

SECTION 1—OBJECT OF THE PAMPHLET

1. The object of this pamphlet is to provide all officers with general information on the Soviet Army in a compact form. Although it has been written with the instructional requirements of Staff Colleges and Schools in mind, it is intended as much for the regimental officer as the staff officer or intelligence officer. It may be used as a basis for lectures to troops.

SECTION 2—GENERAL

2. The tactical chapters in this pamphlet have been based on examples of Soviet operations during the last war, but take into account recent reorganization and current training policy.

Much of the information has been compiled from Russian sources, which are inclined to gloss over the shortcomings of the Soviet army. It should be clearly understood that although certain principles are laid down in Soviet publications, troops in the field may not necessarily succeed in applying them. For example, it is stated in Section 14, para. 2, that rifle divisions may be given final objectives as far inside the enemy defences as 10 miles. This should by no means be taken to imply that they always succeed in attaining these objectives. Wherever possible, however, German information on the Red Army in war has also been studied in order to give a balanced picture of Soviet capabilities on the battle field.

3. The main strength of the Soviet Army lies in its numbers. In World War II the Red Army suffered 13 million casualties in killed or permanently disabled, while the German forces confronting them suffered only four million similar casualties. Despite these very heavy losses the Russian forces on the European front in the final phases of the war still outnumbered the German forces opposing them by over two to one.

The same applied in the case of the Russian air force. They produced a swarm of aircraft over the battle-field, which overwhelmed the German air force by sheer weight of numbers, despite inferior performance.

The Russian soldier, is neither so tough, brave, and frugal, as the Japanese, nor of such a high standard of general technical ability and education as the German. There is no doubt that a well trained British soldier, making full use of the weapons at his disposal, is the superior of his Russian counterpart.

CHAPTER 2

HISTORY OF THE RED ARMY

SECTION 3—THE RED ARMY, 1918-1946

1. The Red Army was formed in February 1918, and was rapidly welded into a competent fighting force. It was initially employed in combating counter-revolutionary activity, and first saw battle during the Polish campaign of 1920.

After the Polish war, Soviet military authorities concentrated upon further development of the Red Army, with the object of making it the largest and most powerful in the world.

Until 1936, a close liaison existed between the Soviet military authorities and the German General Staff, with the result that the Red Army was built up along German lines. This development was seriously retarded by the purge of Marshal Tukachevsky and his associates in 1937, as the former was one of the few influential senior officers who understood modern German tactical doctrine.

2. In November 1939, the Red Army invaded Finland, and the ensuing campaign demonstrated the existence of serious weaknesses. Commanders proved unable to co-ordinate the action of the component parts of their formations; moreover the system of dual control by military and political officers, whereby political commissars had the power to veto all orders, proved to be a failure. Administration was inefficient, equipment, particularly technical equipment, was of poor quality; specialists and technicians were few in number, and of a low standard.

3. Lessons learnt during the campaign were not wasted, and the Soviet High Command immediately began to put matters right. As the standard of training had been found to be poor, manoeuvres in 1940 were carried out on a battalion basis, with the object of building up sound unit tactics, and raising the standard of junior officers. Inefficient commanders were removed, however good their political qualifications, and commissars were deprived of their military powers; their duties were confined to political training and morale. In order to facilitate command the rifle division was reduced in size from a total personnel complement of 19,000 to one of 14,500.

4. The Red Army was still reorganizing when the German and satellite armies invaded the USSR in June 1941. The initial deployment to meet this advance consisted of three main groups of forces, with a small group on the Finnish front. These groupings proved too unwieldy, as the Southern group alone was composed of fifty divisions. Inter group boundaries were badly co-ordinated, a situation of which the Germans took full advantage.

It was largely as a result of this lack of co-ordination, and the fact that many weaknesses disclosed during the Finnish campaign had not been rectified, that the Red Army was compelled to retreat. Moreover, the German Army was at that time well equipped, trained in war, and numerically superior to the Russian forces. Although the Red Army consisted of 186 divisions, only 119 were immediately available to engage 152 axis divisions, of which a very large proportion were German.

However, the German plan was too ambitious, and their various thrusts and pincer movements failed to achieve their objectives by the times laid down by the High Command. This was mainly due to the Germans having underestimated the staunchness of the Red Army forces, who were not dismayed by being encircled, and succeeded in extricating the majority of their formations, though losing a large number of men, much of their equipment, and most of of their armour. The advent of winter compelled the German armies to slow their rate of advance, and finally enabled the Red Army to make a firm stand.

5. A thorough reorganization then took place, and a new policy was conceived, which was implemented during the ensuing years of the war.

The three groups of forces were broken up, and fronts were formed; these fronts were the equivalents of British Army Groups, and were approximately 12 in number, each with an average composition of three rifle armies, one tank army, and one air army. If two or more fronts were to be involved in a single operation then a command team was despatched from Supreme Headquarters in Moscow to co-ordinate their actions. Examples were the operations at Stalingrad, Leningrad, and Berlin, all of which were organized by command teams headed by Marshal Zhukov.

Rifle divisions were reduced in strength to a total of 9,000 and shorn of all unnecessary units, retaining a small proportion of guns and mortars. Artillery was concentrated into formations up to corps strength, and employed under centralized control by fronts and armies, on occasions under the direct control of Supreme Headquarters. At the same time it was progressively motorized.

Equipment was improved in quantity and quality. A particular feature of Soviet administration was to introduce new equipments in large quantities at its initial appearance, simultaneously in all areas.

Military traditions were revived, in order to improve morale, and *élite* formations were introduced. A unit or formation which particularly distinguished itself won the title of "Guards". All personnel of such units received extra pay and better amenities, and personnel transferred to other units retained their guards status. Guards privileges were cancelled if the recipients ceased to maintain the high standard required. Other methods of raising morale were the build-up of patriotism, and the recognition of religion.

An extensive mobilization and training programme was launched, with such success that the Red Army was eventually able to maintain a superiority in men and armour in the proportion of four to one over the Germans on every offensive front.

Rigorous discipline was maintained at all levels, and officers or men who failed to reach the required standard, or committed any misdemeanour were liable for transfer to penal units, several of which existed in every army.

Full use was made of partisans behind the German lines; partisan bands were organized from Moscow, supplied with essentials by air, and acted in co-ordination with operations by the Red Army. Their main tasks were to disorganize the enemy rear, and report on enemy movements.

6. Victory was finally achieved over the German forces through the implementation of this reorganization and policy, through improved Soviet tactics and technique, and as a result of the Allied attacks on Germany.

SECTION 4—CHARACTERISTICS OF THE SOVIET SOLDIER IN BATTLE

1. The Russian soldier is extremely brave in the attack, stubborn in defence, and sets little value upon his own life. In addition to this, he is very tough and is an adept at field-craft, having all the cunning of a hunter. His up-bringing has taught him to be self-reliant and resourceful, to live on the country, and to improvise anything from a sledge to a bridge capable of bearing tanks. Propaganda teaches him to regard an enemy soldier as a personal enemy, rather than the representative of a warring state, and on the strength of this he fights bitterly and ruthlessly.

Despite this natural courage, he is liable to become flustered, and alarmed when he first encounters something that he does not understand, such as a tank attack, bombing and strafing, or an artillery concentration. But he learns how to deal with such situations after a little experience, and then they have less effect upon him than upon more civilized races.

There is a great shortage of technicians in the Soviet Army, and those available are mainly drafted into technical units, such as armour, artillery, engineers, and signals.

There are very few amenities in the Soviet Army, and consequently the administrative tail is considerably less than in most other armies. The Russian soldier is used to frugality and accepts it without complaining, as he has never known better conditions.

2. Officers have been brought up under similar conditions to the men, though a new officer class, specially trained and selected, is now beginning to appear. The majority of officers are painstakingly thorough, but are inclined to be slow, and lacking in initiative. As a result, all authority is centralized, and senior officers, such as corps and army commanders take too great a share in actual manoeuvre of sub-units. But a proportion of officers, particularly at the highest levels, are both thorough and brilliant, and this proportion will increase as

time goes on. Most officers at present have battle experience, and have proved themselves adequate; no good officers have been demobilized.

3. Examples of Russian bravery and toughness, quoted from German sources, are as follows:—

(a) *Physical toughness.* A Red Army rifle battalion attacked the outskirts of Medin at dawn in January 1942, in a temperature of minus 43 degrees Fahrenheit. After heavy casualties, the attack came to a standstill on a snowfield, no further movement being possible. The survivors remained lying motionless in the snow for 10 hours, without any special protection from the cold, and then renewed the attack at dusk with shouts of "Hurrah!"

(b) *Fighting despite privation.* A Red Army task force, which had broken through the German line in wooded country, avoided all German attempts to destroy it for 12 days, and made seven attempts to break out. On the thirteenth day, the task force, consisting of 60 men, was surrounded and annihilated. It had, without any supplies, and without facilities for keeping a fire going, fed itself on only the bark of trees, fir shoots, and snow.

(c) *Effect of propaganda.* A reconnaissance pilot shot down at Yukknov in the spring of 1942, landed by parachute in the street. He immediately opened up vigorous tommy-gun fire on German soldiers running towards him, and forced them to attack in a regular manner, employing mortars. After wounding six Germans, he shot himself through the head with one of his last bullets, to avoid capture.

CHAPTER 3

COMMAND AND CONTROL

SECTION 5—THE HIGH COMMAND

Higher control of the armed forces by the State.

1. The ultimate governing body in the Soviet Union is the Supreme Soviet of the USSR presided over by Shvernik, President of the USSR. Composed of two elected chambers, the Soviet of the Union and the Soviet of Nationalities, this body has certain superficial resemblances to the British Parliament, although its powers are limited to ratification and it meets only biannually. Between sessions its powers are delegated to the Praesidium, a body elected by the two chambers of the Supreme Soviet sitting in joint session.

Subordinate to the Supreme Soviet is the Council of Ministers, which is a body composed of the heads of all the Ministries (both Union Republican and All Union) presided over by Stalin. The most important Ministers (for instance, those of Foreign Affairs, Foreign Trade, and the Armed Forces) hold the appointment of Vice-President of the Council of Ministers, which gives them an element of authority over the other Ministries. This "inner cabinet" of the Council of Ministers corresponds closely to the Politburo and is the body which, in fact, governs the USSR.

Control of the armed forces by the State is exercised through the Minister of the Armed Forces, Marshal Bulganin, who is an officer with political rather than military background. He was appointed in February 1947, and took over his appointment from Marshal Stalin, who had held the appointment of People's Commissar for Defence during the War.

Set-up and organization of the armed forces.

2. The end of the war found the armed forces of the Soviet Union organized in two People's Commissariats, one for the Navy and one for Defence. The People's Commissariat for the Navy had its own air element integrated into it, and was entirely self-supporting in every respect.

The People's Commissariat for Defence embraced the Red Army and its integrated air element, and included the administrative and surveillance organizations of the Red Army.

By a major reorganization of the High Command in February 1946, the two People's Commissariats were abolished and were replaced by a single unified command, now known as the Ministry of the Armed Forces (MVS). At the same time the Air Forces were separated from the two senior services and were formed into a separate arm of equal status with the Army and the Navy under the Ministry of the Armed Forces. The supply and administrative directorates of all three services were placed under a unified control known as the Rear of the Armed Forces. Five deputy Ministers were appointed, the first being the then Chief of the General Staff of the Armed Forces, Marshal Vasilevski, and the other four being the heads of the three services and of the Rear (Marshal Konev for the Land Forces, Admiral of Fleet Yumashev for for the Navy, Marshal of Aviation Vershinin for the Air Force and Army General Khrulev for the Rear). A sixth, the Inspector General (Marshal Govorov) has subsequently been appointed. Certain directorates with interests in two or more services (for instance the Chief Directorate of the Commander of Artillery of the Armed Forces, the Directorate of Airborne Troops and the Chief Political Directorate) have remained under the direct control of the Ministry.

The counter-espionage organization within the Armed Forces (GUKR "Smersh") has reverted to the control of the Ministry of State Security (MGB) in name as well as in fact, and is believed now to be called OKR MGB (Otdyel Kontrrazvedki MGB—Counter-Espionage Section, MGB). Political surveillance is still an integral part of the armed forces organization, but the Political Directorate has its own chain of command and information, which is independent of the military commanders at all levels, and is ultimately responsible to the Central Committee of the All-Union Communist Party.

Conclusion.

3. The reorganization of the Soviet High Command has resulted in a greater equality between the three services. Although the Soviet Army is still regarded as the senior and most important service, the splitting off of the Air Force has increased the latter's importance and standing, while the Navy now no longer runs the danger of being regarded as a Cinderella to the Army. A unified command implies a pooling of resources in lines of research and experiment, a uniformity of equipment and a closer understanding between the Services. A single organization in charge of rear Services implies a great saving in manpower through the elimination of lines of communication and administration and a greater flexibility in the use of reserves of equipment and supply. Weaknesses in this organization would only appear as the result of a war, but so far as can be judged it is a sound and coordinated structure which should make for greater efficiency.

The breakdown of Ministry of Armed Forces is attached at Appendix 'A'.

SECTION 6—MILITARY DISTRICTS

1. The USSR is divided into 21 military districts, which can be roughly compared with commands in England. A military district is commanded by a senior general, or sometimes a marshal, who has authority over all personnel in the district irrespective of their service, and is directly subordinate to the Ministry of the Armed Forces.

2 The district commander is assisted by a War Council, composed of a maximum of five, including:—
- (a) The Secretary of the Regional Communist Party.
- (b) A senior political commander.
- (c) Two commanders of the principal arms, such as artillery and engineers.

At least one member of the War Council must countersign all orders. Senior commanders of supporting arms and services ranks as deputy commanders for their particular spheres, whether they are members of the War Council or not.

3. The status of a military district is equivalent to that of a group of forces in occupied territory, and to the war-time front, but it is not operational in character. Its functions include the following:—
- (a) Conscription and induction of personnel called up each year, for all three services.
- (b) Administration of reservists.
- (c) Raising of new formations.
- (d) Mobilization.
- (e) Requisitioning of transport and supplies in war.
- (f) Liaison with anti-aircraft defence districts (PVO).

(g) Liaison with governments of Soviet Socialists Republics on matters of military importance such as Osoaviakhim, an organization which deals with military training of the civilian population, and service reservists.
(h) Control and supervision of military formations, schools and academies within its boundaries.
(j) Security within the district.
(k) Training of all formations under command.
(l) Defence plans for the district.
(m) Political indoctrination.

SECTION 7—POLITICAL CONTROL IN THE ARMED FORCES

1. Great importance is attached to political training in the Soviet Army and much time is devoted to it. The political organization exists as an integral part of the army, to disseminate communist propaganda, and to educate the troops along orthodox communist lines. This organization consists of the following personnel, or bodies of personnel.

Deputy Commanders for Political Affairs.

2. These exist at all levels and are the personal advisers on political matters to commanders of all formations down to and including the battalion. Their chain of command runs parallel to the military chain of command. Before and during the early part of the war they had the power of vetoing the orders of the military commanders, even on military matters. This was found to be an unsuccessful method of conducting affairs and the Political Commissars, as they were then known, had their powers curtailed so that they could not interfere with the conduct of purely military operations. This happened first during the Finnish campaign in February 1941; later in 1941 these powers were regranted owing to the initial German successes and resulting lowering of morale. In 1942 their powers were again curtailed at about the time of the Stalingrad battle, and were never again re-granted. In 1943 they ceased to be called Political Commissars and received their present titles of Deputy Commanders for Political Affairs.

Their chief duties may be summarized as follows:—
(a) Direction and control of Communist party and Komsomol members in the formations under their control.
(b) Education of all ranks.
(c) Publication and issue of all newspapers.
(d) Issuing the 'correct' interpretation of news.
(e) Passing on to all ranks the views and doctrines of the Communist party.
(f) Welfare.
(g) Entertainment, cinemas, concerts, libraries etc.
(h) Sport.

(j) They may also be regarded as 'Atheistic padres', for example, they bury the dead. As far as is known they do not perform marriages, but undoubtedly would play a considerable part in the arrangements.

It should be remembered that many of these duties are complementary for example, education, entertainments, and news broadcasts are closely tied up with the dissemination of political doctrine.

Communist Party.

3. Members of the Communist party form cells in the Soviet Army in all units down to company level. Each cell of more than 15 members organizes an office from which propaganda, news, etc., is disseminated under the supervision of the Chief of Party Cell Office. The party members also regard themselves as helpers of the military commander, and pride themselves on setting an example of military zeal and efficiency. In battle they must always be in the lead and exhort their fellows to greater deeds. Their losses in the late war were enormous and their decoration rate was also high.

4. A further function of the party organization is the enrolment of new members. It should be emphasized that though entrance to the party was easy during the war, it is not at all easy in normal times. To join the party a man must be proposed by three independent party members of not less than three years standing, each of whom must have known him personally for at least one year. They must vouch for his political reliability and the orthodoxy of his views. He then becomes a probationary member for a period of one year, during which time he may attend all party meetings and may voice his opinions but may not vote. If he successfully completes his year of probation he becomes a fully fledged party member of a desirable state. Membership of the party is virtually essential for any kind of successful career. The lower age limit for fully party membership is 18 years, and expulsion from the party is regarded as damning.

Komsomol.

5. This is the name for the Communist youth organization; the upper age limit is 25, unless an individual holds some office in the organization which renders it desirable that he should continue after that age. Its activities are much the same as those of the Communist party proper, and normally members graduate to the party on reaching the age of 18 to 20 years. Membership of the Komsomol does away with the year's probationary membership of the party proper, and recommendation by a Komsomol cell takes the place of the recommendation of one of the full members when a man is proposed for membership of the party. Komsomol activities are closely supervised by the party members, and Komsomol members may attend party meetings without the right of voting. The aims, objects, ideas, and codes of the

Komsomol are identical with those of the party proper; the lower age limit is not known but is thought to be about 9 to 10 years. A possible bar to membership would be political unreliability of parents, but otherwise the organization can be easily joined.

Conclusions.

6. When it is considered that Communist Party cells exist down to company level and that the Komsomol organization exists in addition to this, it can be seen that the political control of the army is extremely strong. This renders it very difficult for the soldiers to be subverted by any influences other than those acceptable to the Soviet State. All news, entertainment, literature, and indeed conversation is controlled and coloured according to the current party line, right down to the private soldier.

CHAPTER 4

POST-WAR REORGANIZATION OF THE SOVIET ARMY

SECTION 8—GENERAL

1. The Soviet Army received its present title in 1946, when it was reorganized along modern lines, with the object of making its basic formations flexible, hard-hitting, and mobile. It is now composed of rifle armies, sometimes known as shock armies, and mechanized armies.

Rifle armies normally contain three rifle corps, each of either three rifle divisions, or of two rifle divisions and one mechanized division.

The mechanized army is a formation which was newly created in 1946. It has no corps formations, and is composed of two tank divisions and two mechanized divisions.

Both rifle and mechanized armies hold, in addition to the above, artillery divisions, engineer, signal, and administrative formations. Airborne and cavalry formations may be placed under the command of armies for specific operations, but are normally retained under more centralized command.

About half the divisions in the Soviet peace-time army are rifle divisions; about a quarter are either tank or mechanized divisions; the remainder are made up of artillery and cavalry divisions.

The existence of airborne formations larger than brigade in the peace-time army is doubtful.

Organization charts are attached at Appendices D to Q.

SECTION 9—SOVIET ARMY DIVISIONS

1. The Soviet Army has a strength in peace-time of some two and a half million men. On mobilization this figure could probably be doubled in a month.

The rifle division.

2. Organic transport in the rifle division will eventually be motorized, but the transition from horse-drawn equipment is taking place slowly. No vehicles are allotted for carrying riflemen, who normally march, but a rifle division up to establishment in MT can be made fully mobile by an allotment of TCVs from an army pool.

When reorganization has been completed, rifle divisions will contain a medium tank self-propelled gun regiment, which, together with self-propelled gun troops in rifle regiments, gives the division a strength in armour of 52 medium tanks and 34 self-propelled guns.

The mechanized division.

3. All transport in the mechanized division is motorized, and all personnel are carried in unit vehicles. It exemplifies the Soviet doctrine that infantry and armour should work together, as each mechanized regiment contains two rifle battalions and one tank battalion; moreover, both the medium tank regiment and the heavy tank self-propelled gun regiment contain a motorized rifle battalion.

The artillery is lacking in flat trajectory weapons, as their task will be carried out by tanks and self-propelled guns. The mortar regiment will probably be used to protect tank harbours against infantry attack, from positions inside the perimeter.

The tank division.

4. The tank division is a highly mobile armoured formation, with sufficient motorized infantry for its own protection and to hold ground captured by tanks. It contains one more medium tank battalion, and only one less rifle battalion than the mechanized division, but the armour is concentrated; otherwise, the organization is very similar to that of the mechanized division.

Artillery divisions.

5. (a) Artillery divisions are formations whose establishment is liable to change to suit particular tasks. A typical organization might be:—
One 122-mm howitzer brigade.
One 152-mm howitzer brigade.
One 203-mm howitzer brigade.
One rocket launcher brigade (30-cm rocket launchers).
One 160-mm mortar brigade.

The strength in personnel of such a division would be between 9,000 and 12,000.

(b) Anti-aircraft divisions, with personnel strengths of approximately 2,500, are included among the number of artillery divisions, and contain two 37-mm light anti-aircraft regiments and two anti-aircraft regiments armed with 85-mm guns.

Cavalry divisions.

6. Cavalry divisions still exist, but will probably only be used in country or climatic conditions unsuited to armour, and in patrolling or raiding capacity. Personnel are taught to fight on horseback, or on foot as infantry.

Armour.

7. The Soviet Army is strong in tanks and self-propelled guns; if all rifle divisions of the peace-time army were deployed in line, with tank and mechanized divisions sited in rear, the average support available for one rifle division, including its own weapons, would be 200 tanks or self-propelled guns, and 80 armoured cars or carriers. After mobilization the proportion will probably be less, as a greater proportion of new rifle divisions than tank and mechanized divisions will be formed.

SECTION 10—DIVISIONAL AND UNIT STAFFS

1. Divisional staffs of all types throughout the Soviet Army appear to be organized on a similar basis, with the following exceptions:—
   (a) Tank and mechanized divisions have additional technical staff and include a colonel (technical).
   (b) AA divisions are commanded by colonels, and have a large technical element. The actual numerical strength of the headquarter staff is very close to that of the other divisions.

2. Regiments and brigades are commanded by colonels. Staff organizations are very similar throughout with exceptions as in para. 1 above. Tank regiments include a major (technical) in the regimental staff.

3. (a) Battalions are usually commanded by lieutenant colonels.
   (b) Rifle battalions and artillery batteries are commanded by majors, except for rocket launcher batteries, which may be commanded by lieutenant colonels, and have majors as chiefs of staff.
   (c) Companies are commanded by captains.
   (d) Platoons and artillery sections are commanded by lieutenants.

4. The detailed organization of divisional, regimental, and battalion staffs, in a rifle division are shown in Appendices S and T.

CHAPTER 5

TACTICS—THE OFFENSIVE

SECTION 11—MAJOR OFFENSIVES

1. Major offensives are carried out by groups of fronts, an average front consisting of four rifle or mechanized armies, and one air army. Operations are controlled and co-ordinated by command teams under the orders of the high command, and normally take the form of either encirclement, or forward thrusts.

2. Encirclement operations are usually carried out by two fronts, occasionally assisted by a third during the final phases. Rifle armies of each front breach the enemy line on the flanks of the group which they intend to surround; mechanized formations then advance through the gap, and execute a pincer movement. Reserve rifle formations move forward and take over from the mechanized units the task of hemming in the enemy, forming an inner perimeter. Mechanized forces then fight their way outwards in order to establish an outer perimeter, at a distance of about 50 miles from the inner perimeter. When the outer perimeter is firm, the operation for liquidating the encircled enemy begins; enemy forces which succeed in breaking out through the inner perimeter have little chance of reaching the outer perimeter before being destroyed.

3. Forward thrusts by a front entail breaching the enemy line at several places, isolating groups, and destroying them individually. Having broken through, and having obtained room to manoeuvre, the attack is developed by armoured formations to a depth of 200 miles, with the object of defeating enemy strategic reserves in detail, before they can influence the battle. Three or more fronts may combine to launch simultaneous forward thrusts in the same direction.

SECTION 12—THE ADVANCE TO CONTACT AND ENCOUNTER BATTLE

Preparation.

1. The staff make a full appreciation before the commencement of an advance, and every effort is made to ensure that information is up to date. Whenever possible, road reconnaissance parties are sent out, in addition to air reconnaissance. Such parties might consist of an operations staff officer, representatives of all arms with a strong engineer element, and an escort.

2. When the spearhead of the advance is an armoured unit, special detachments are sent on ahead to arrange freedom of movement for the advancing formations. The duties of these detachments include:—

(a) Obtaining information about the enemy.
(b) Road reconnaissance.

(c) Suggestions for a suitable order of march for the main body.
(d) Repairing roads and bridges.
(e) Clearance of obstacles.
(f) Making diversions where necessary.

A detachment working on the main axis of advance is entirely motorized, consisting of up to one company of engineers, escorted by infantry, armoured cars tanks, and self-propelled artillery.

These detachments move in tactical bounds, about 15 miles in length. Parties are detached to deal with obstacles as they are encountered, until the whole detachment is employed.

Armoured fighting vehicles patrol between working parties, but the majority of the armour is held concentrated under the detachment commander at the most vulnerable, or important position. If the column is attacked, tanks counter-attack, in order that engineer work may proceed without interruption for as long as possible.

Advance guard.

3. Tasks of the advance guards include the following:—
(a) Capturing and holding tactical features until the arrival of the main forces.
(b) Shielding the advance of the main forces.
(c) Reconnaissance to find out the composition, grouping, and general condition of the enemy, also the nature of his fieldworks and defences.
(d) Information and detail of enemy reinforcements.
(e) Capture of aerodromes.

4. The advance is carried out in bounds, from one tactical objective to the next. Advanced detachments are occasionally sent forward to seize and hold specific features until the arrival of the vanguard. These objectives may be road junctions, natural obstacles, and defiles.

The frontage of the advance will vary according to different situations. A mechanized division might advance along one main axis, or on a front of six or seven miles, with an armoured group on each flank, and two mechanized regiments, on separate routes, in the centre.

Advance guards will normally be portions of either tank, or mechanized divisions, though occasions may arise when the leading formation may be from a rifle, or cavalry division. There may be one or more axis of advance; when a column consists partly of marching infantry, and partly of mechanical vehicles, the vehicles are usually kept in an echelon apart, on a separate route.

Vanguard.

5. The distance of the vanguard from the main body will depend upon the situation, but it must ensure security of movement, timely deployment, and timely joining of battle, for the main body.

The leading element is normally a detachment of motor cyclists from the divisional reconnaissance battalion.

6. When the leading formation is a mechanized division, the vanguard will probably be based on a motorized rifle battalion, with artillery, tanks, self-propelled guns, and mortars, under command. An engineer element is usually included for removal of obstacles, and assisting armoured fighting vehicles over difficult ground.

When a tank division is in the lead, the vanguard will probably consist of a medium tank battalion, with a company of infantry, a detachment of self-propelled artillery, or anti-tank guns, and engineers.

A proportion of infantry ride on the tanks, in order to be immediately available for their support.

Main body.

7. The main body is based on a mechanized regiment for a mechanized division, and on a medium tank regiment for a tank division. It follows close behind the vanguard, sometimes only three miles behind. A proportion of the tanks, self-propelled guns, and artillery are distributed throughout the column, but three-quarters of the fire support is concentrated under the column commander for use as a reserve.

Light anti-aircraft guns are either divided throughout the column, or moved independently in bounds for the protection of defiles.

Bridging material is carried when there is a possibility of encountering water obstacles.

Heavy tanks do not normally form part of the advance guard, but when they are included, they travel one or two miles in rear of the column.

8. When the advance guard is based on a rifle division, the motorized echelon, which will consist largely of artillery, either moves on a parallel route, or in advance of the marching infantry. This echelon is escorted by a proportion of infantry, tanks, self-propelled guns, and light anti-aircraft weapons, and is prepared to fight a delaying action if necessary.

The marching column advances in the normal manner.

Cavalry is only of use in country unsuitable for tanks and vehicles.

Headquarters.

9. Commanders usually move at the head of the main body of their formations, frequently in tanks. Unit representatives, representatives of supporting arms, and air liaison officers move in groups close behind commanders.

When contact has been made, the commander immediately selects an observation post, from which he can best make his appreciation for the next phase of the battle.

During the attack, commanders of tank and mechanized units are located behind the tank units operating at the point of main effort.

Main headquarters travels behind the combatant units, in the rear of the main body.

B

Rate of advance.

10. Standard rates of movement when an advance is unopposed are approximately as follows:—

(a) Infantry . . . . 2½ miles per hour.
(b) Motorized transport . . . . 10 to 12½ ,, ,, ,,
(c) Tanks and tractor drawn artillery 5 to 7 ,, ,, ,,

Protection against ground attack.

11. When contact is anticipated, strong march protection is essential. For this purpose, vanguards, advance guards, and flank guards are reinforced by artillery and anti-tank weapons. Chemical warfare detachments are distributed throughout the columns, and commanders retain a strong mobile reserve of engineers.

Ground protection is primarily achieved by means of points, usually consisting of two tanks, carrying infantry. These points travel in front, in rear, and to the flanks of an advancing unit. Flank points normally work at a distance of one or two miles from the main body, but work closer in if the country is wooded or otherwise enclosed, and are augmented in fire power.

On occasions, flank protection may be achieved by a series of fixed piquets on heights and road junctions. They are sent out in advance of the main force, and withdraw as it passes. These piquets are usually reinforced with anti-tank guns.

Particular attention is paid to anti-tank defence, and every advancing force contains a large proportion of self-propelled artillery, or anti-tank guns, occasionally both. A battalion group for example, might include an additional anti-tank battery and a troop of self-propelled guns.

Protection against air attack.

12. An allotment of anti-aircraft artillery is considered essential for every advancing force, and moves in tactical bounds for the protection of defiles. If the route is uniform throughout, a proportion is allotted to the advance group, the main forces, and the artillery echelon.

Marching units have personnel trained as spotters, and detachments are allotted to open fire at attacking aircraft.

Anti-aircraft, anti-tank, and anti-gas weapons must be in a state of constant readiness, and all units must be constantly prepared for air or ground attack.

Concealment.

13. Special attention is paid to concealment on the march, even to the extent of frequently appending a special march deception plan to movement orders. This deception is carried out by a variety of means, such as disguising tanks and guns as lorries by means of wooden super-structures, and by executing feint marches on different routes.

On occasions the order of march is completely changed during the course of movement.

Camouflage is carefully applied at halts during the day-time, and full advantage is taken of natural cover.

All troops are given intensive instruction and training in night marches. During offensive operations armoured units push forward night and day, refuelling and maintaining their vehicles at first light, but ensuring that reconnaissance is continued by some portion of the force. They endeavour to maintain continuous contact, once contact has been made. Cases are known of tanks carrying out an offensive advance on rainy nights, along unknown roads.

Communications.

14. During the advance, wireless is normally used by reconnaissance elements only. Other orders are given verbally to unit representatives, or sent by liaison officers and despatch riders.

Wireless traffic begins as soon as an advance guard deploys, and is maintained until line has been laid.

Commanders normally have a long range wireless set, in addition to their unit set, for direct communication with their higher formation.

Direct contact with supporting aircraft is obtained by means of air liaison officers.

The encounter battle.

15. First contact is usually made by means of air attacks on enemy columns, with the main effort directed against tanks and artillery. Subsequently, long range artillery may be used to shell defiles.

Immediately physical contact has been made, leading elements push on as far as possible, overcoming minor resistance, and then take steps to obtain information about the enemy, with particular reference to:—

(a) Anti-tank defences.
(b) Grouping.
(c) Flanks.
(d) Fire power and armour.
(e) Weak sectors.

Prisoners are considered to be a valuable source of information.

16. The procedure adopted on contact varies according to the following situations:—

(a) If the enemy have not had time to deploy.
(b) If the enemy has already deployed.
(c) If the enemy is already occupying a defensive position.

In the first case, it is usually considered best to attack, as, even if the assault fails, valuable information is obtained.

In the second and third cases, commanders have to decide whether to launch an immediate attack from the line of march, a quickly mounted attack after further reconnaissance and regrouping, or a deliberate attack after the arrival of reinforcements. Great stress is laid on the fact that an unsuccessful attack may result in considerable delay to the main forces, and that in the third situation it may often be advisable to await reinforcements, and then strike a decisive blow, rather than to make an abortive assault.

17. If the enemy are still an the march, the vanguard endeavours to forward enemy units, while tanks engage the main body, and the artillery.

Attempts are made to split up the enemy column, and destroy isolated elements individually. No time is wasted in complete regrouping, or centralizing control over fire power, but artillery fire power and air attacks are developed gradually throughout the attack, as they become available.

Infantry is deployed as close to the enemy, and in as much depth, as is possible, and artillery is brought into action from the line of march. If strong anti-tank defences have been located, tanks may not be used in the first wave of the attack. In this case, the leading company of infantry carries out a methodical advance until held up, when it digs itself in. Other companies then stage attacks from the flanks and the rear some of which may be feints. The maximum use is made of self-propelled guns, and direct support by artillery and mortars.

18. If the enemy has already deployed, the vanguard holds its ground while the main body of the advance guard deploys. An attack is launched as soon as possible, usually preceded by an air strike.

If the enemy possesses armour, efforts are made to separate the infantry from the tanks, with the support of artillery fire, and under cover of an anti-tank screen, unless the enemy tank force is considered to be inferior. If such is the case, a direct attack is launched, usually headed by tanks, and followed up by infantry. Where a strong enemy anti-tank screen has been located, tanks attack together with infantry, but not as the leading echelon.

19. If the enemy is already occupying a defensive position, further reconnaissance is carried out, and special observer groups may be sent forward, consisting of engineers with signal personnel for communication. Observation posts are established, and mast periscopes may be used, if available.

The infantry is then regrouped and the artillery brought under centralized control. Tanks are concentrated by way of concealed approaches, or under cover of darkness, and arrangements are made for air support.

The time taken to launch a quickly mounted attack by any group up to the strength of a division is calculated to be a minimum of five to six hours of daylight, and a maximum of 24 hours. An attack on a corps level would require a minimum of 8 to 10 hours of daylight for preparation but the maximum time limit remains unchanged.

20. If the enemy proves to be superior, vanguards endeavour to hold sufficient ground to cover the deployment of the main body, but if they

are compelled to give ground, the main body deploys on the nearest suitable tactical feature. The same ruling applies with relation to the advance guard and the main forces.

Leading armoured units frequently withdraw, as part of a deception plan to lead their pursuers into ambushes of self-propelled guns or heavy tanks.

Artillery in the advance to contact.

21. The main fire power of the vanguard is provided by self-propelled artillery, which is employed in a variety of roles.

If the infantry is without tanks, light or medium self-propelled guns are used in support, but in this case they are always provided with an infantry escort. Their tasks are to give fire support to the advance group, to protect the deployment of the main body, and to act in an anti-tank role.

When the infantry is supported by tanks, the main task of the self-propelled artillery is to protect and support the tanks. For this duty heavy self-propelled guns are usually employed, in order to deal with enemy armour which is beyond the scope of medium tanks. In this case, owing to limited ammunition, they do not engage targets that can be neutralized by tanks or infantry. They do, however, engage pill-boxes, and anti-tank strong points, occasionally in co-operation with field artillery.

Light self-propelled artillery is usually employed in a concentrated role, but is occasionally divided into troops for support of individual units, or to give a false impression of an advance on a broad front.

Other types of self-propelled artillery are usually employed with individual tank units, but are always liable to be subordinated to a central headquarters if it should become necessary to bring down a heavy concentration of fire.

Heavy and medium self-propelled artillery in support of tanks follows close behind the battle formations, and concentrate their fire on strong points while the tanks manoeuvre. Fire is brought down by observation, without previous reference to tank commanders. Self-propelled gun detachments indicate targets to each other by wireless, followed by a shot at the target.

When tanks encounter superior armour, they usually withdraw through self-propelled artillery, a proportion of whom are usually able to prepare an ambush.

Self-propelled artillery is nearly always provided with infantry protection and engineer assistance.

22. Corps artillery is allotted to divisions for movement, but can only be deployed and brought into action with the consent of the corps commander. This includes the corps anti-tank reserve, which usually consists of one regiment.

In the case of mechanized armies, which have no corps formations, army artillery is allotted to divisions in a similar manner.

Air support.

23. Air support is considered to be an essential feature of all offensive operations. During an advance, support is usually provided by the entire front line air force, and tasks include:

(a) Destruction of targets interfering with the advance of armoured units, and columns on the march.

(b) Engaging enemy reserves.

(c) Maintaining continuous air cover over advancing mobile formations.

(d) Reconnaissance.

Air liaison officers accompany commanders of advanced groups, who can either call for air support from forward aerodromes, or can direct aircraft overhead on to specific targets.

Communicaton with air headquarters is maintained by wireless, line, or despatch-carrying aircraft. Direct communication from ground to air is carried out by wireless, rockets, smoke, or ground strips.

Aircraft indicate targets to each other by wireless speech in clear rockets, smoke, or by fire on the targets.

Airfield construction units follow up with second line mobile troops to prepare or recondition airfields.

Administration.

24. All supplies are increased in quantity in anticipation of an advance. Divisional supply units and installations are moved forward in echelons, either as part of the regimental and battalion supply columns or as separate echelons.

At the commencement of the encounter battle; ammunition echelons, the main dressing station, and transport for the evacuation of wounded, are moved forward.

Tank units are accompanied by large tankers with fuel reserves.

SECTION 13—PREPARATION FOR A MAJOR OFFENSIVE

Reconnaissance.

1. In the last war, preparations for a major offensive took from two to four months, during which time the Russians usually succeeded in pin-pointing most German positions in the area visible from their own lines. This was achieved mainly by a co-ordinated network of observation posts, continually manned by specially trained personnel, and partly by other means, such as patrolling and aerial photography. Feint attacks and decoy tanks were often used to draw enemy fire, and thereby assess the defensive fire plan.

Patrolling, fieldcraft, and camouflage are of a very high standard; there have been occasions when an entire Soviet battalion has infiltrated through German defences by day, and by night, without being perceived until they attacked from inside the position.

Reconnaissance in force may be carried out by battalion, or even regimental attacks with armoured and artillery support, two or three days before the main assault; any success achieved during such reconnaissance is immediately exploited.

Planning and command.

2. Planning is carried out in great detail, covering all phases of a battle, including pursuit, but is seldom flexible. Commanders prefer a rigid plan, rather than to trust the initiative of their subordinates in dealing with unforeseen situations, or the efficacy of their communications for controlling a battle. But in order to cope with unforeseen circumstances, commanders themselves are invariably well forward to observe the battle-field. The tactical headquarters of a rifle corps may be sited 1,000 yards from the front line, and divisional command posts even closer.

Deception is a major consideration in planning at all levels, and the endurance and cunning of the Soviet soldier is fully exploited to achieve surprise by attack over difficult ground, and under rigorous climatic conditions.

Troops taking part in an attack are given extensive training over replicas of the actual enemy positions, in exercises with and without live ammunition. Affiliations are the same as they will be in battle, and each unit trains for the specific task allotted to it.

Assembly.

3. Assembly of army troops and rear installations begins up to two months before a major offensive, and takes place 30 to 40 miles behind the front line. Combatant troops move up to areas about five miles in rear of the front line two weeks before the assault, and concentration of all arms is usually completed three days before.

A superiority in armour and personnel of four to one at the point, or points, chosen for breaching the enemy positions is aimed at, and an artillery fire power of 250 guns or mortars to 1,000 yards. Other sectors are often recklessly denuded to achieve this object.

Camouflage and security measures are carefully organized, and equipment difficult to conceal, such as bridging material, is usually collected in a sector adjacent to that from which the offensive is to be launched. German reconnaissance aircraft had considerable difficulty in spotting Russian concentrations, even when specifically searching for them.

Artillery emplacements and OPs are constructed some time before they are to be occupied, not only in the attacking sector, but also in adjacent sectors. Dummies are often constructed on a large scale. The appearance of heavy anti-aircraft guns in the forward areas usually heralds an attack.

Clearance of obstacles.

4. Reconnaissance for obstacles is normally carried out by sapper parties specially allotted to forward units for the purpose; but all units are trained to carry out this task, should the necessity arise. A co-ordinated plan for clearing and breaching obstacles is made at division or even corps level, and issued to units concerned. Commanders then carry out a final reconnaissance on the ground to arrange exact details.

5. Some obstacles are cleared by gun-fire during the artillery preparation, and others by self-propelled guns, or by engineer and infantry storm groups during the assault. In the case of wire obstacles in the latter stage, the usual impromtu means such as mats, coats, and ladders, are employed. Each platoon carries a grapnel attached to 30 to 40 yards of rope, which is used to drag away wire obstacles that are suspected of containing mines or booby traps. Another method is to shower hand-grenades upon the obstacles, in the hope of detonating even anti-tank mines. But engineer groups do carry mine detectors for detailed clearance, and roller tanks are used if available.

Other obstacles, which can be cleared or breached without forfeiting surprise, are dealt with on the night before the attack.

6. One passage is normally made through an obstacle for each rifle and tank platoon, seldom less than two for a rifle company. Sometimes one passage is allotted for the use of both infantry and tanks; when this is the case the infantry and tank commanders make their personal reconnaissance together, and decide the following:—

(a) Allocation of work between sappers, infantry, and tanks.

(b) Covering fire for sappers.

(c) Time by which passages must be completed.

(d) Method of marking.

(e) RVs where units will meet guides.

7. Shortly before the attack is due to be launched, tanks advance rom the rear along previously marked routes, and are met by guides in the immediate rear of the infantry positions. They are then escorted:—

(a) Through own rear minefields. Passages are usually prepared at night, two or three nights before the attack, in order that the last night may be devoted to clearing passages in enemy obstacles. They are carefully guarded, and covered by fire; some mines and knife rests are kept immediately available to fill the gaps in case of enemy attack.

(b) Through own infantry defended areas. Light bridges are provided across trenches and anti-tank ditches.

(c) Through own forward obstacles and minefields.

(d) Over the intervening ground to the enemy forward obstacle belt. The route is usually marked by signs visible only to advancing troops.

(e) Through passages in the enemy obstacle belt. The sappers who cleared the lanes normally take over escort duties at this point. Entrances to lanes are very carefully marked with different signs for each unit whenever possible. Boundaries of the lanes may be marked by flags, signs, or even tripods made of poles. The latter method is often used in winter. Passages are usually made 10 to 12 yards wide initially, but are widened as soon as possible, normally after the leading battalions have passed.

8. Rifle platoons in the assault pass through passages in threes, and extend afterwards into line, with six to eight paces between individuals.

Deployment for attack.

9. Formations are usually deployed for attack with two units forward and one in reserve. Armour for close support moves forward to the line start during artillery preparation, by a previously reconnoitred route.

The frontage of a rifle division is usually one to two miles, a regimental frontage 500 to 1,000 yards, and that of a battalion 400 to 500 yards. Reserve battalions are usually 500 yards in rear of leading battalions, and reserve regiments 1,000 yards in rear. Reserve divisions of a rifle corps are usually 1,500 yards behind the leading divisions.

Artillery Preparation.

10. Artillery preparation normally lasts for approximately two hours, with the object of neutralizing all enemy defended areas to a depth of 4,000 yards, with a simultaneous destructive programme for all known strong points and gun positions. Towards the end of the preparatory period, concentrations are laid down with increased intensity on the forward areas, and rocket salvoes are superimposed over gun and mortar tasks.

11. Counter-battery work during the last war was usually haphazard and ineffective against guns which were not visible to ground observation. A concentration of three Soviet troops upon one enemy troop was considered sufficient for neutralization.

Moderate success was obtained with sound ranging.

SECTION 14—THE ASSAULT

1. Russians usually attacked the Germans in mass formation, making as much noise as possible, both by firing and shouting. As a result, they normally achieved their objectives by sheer weight of numbers, apart from other considerations. When considering Soviet successes, it must be remembered that the Soviet army suffered nearly

14 million military casualties in killed or permanently disabled, but exclusive of prisoners, during the war; while similar German losses on the Eastern Front were probably less than four million.

In future, attacking formations will probably adopt greater dispersion, with six to eight paces between individuals.

The attack.

2. A rifle division may be given final objectives up to 10 miles inside the enemy position. The assault is made on a narrow front in depth; forward elements advance as rapidly as possible to these objectives, while others fan out and widen the breach. The impetus of the attack is progressively increased; as the advance proceeds, and the breach is widened, so the number of units committed is increased, and a greater pressure is put upon the defenders.

To achieve this object, troops are echeloned in waves; the leading wave presses on regardless of casualties, destroying the enemy directly in its path, but by-passing strong points, which are dealt with by following waves. Enemy fire from the flanks is neutralized by artillery concentrations.

When a wave is held up, the next wave either reinforces it, or passes through it. Disciplinary action is taken against commanders who fail to reach their objectives without very strong reasons for failure.

3. Tanks and self-propelled guns accompany the infantry, and, together with low-flying aircraft, support them by fire against unsilenced strong-points. Infantry, some of whom ride on the tanks, are allotted to accompany them as a protection against tank-hunting parties, and anti-tank guns. The first wave of tanks usually moves ahead of the infantry, who follow close behind, intermingled with the second tank wave. Self-propelled guns move in tactical bounds about 300 yards in rear of the leading tanks, to destroy undamaged strong points or anti-tank guns, and to provide flank protection against counter-attack. Heavy tanks are aften allotted when the enemy anti-tank defences are strong.

Reorganization and counter-attack.

4. Some reorganization is carried out at every halt, as the attacking forces advance through the enemy defences in tactical bounds. After attaining the objective, or being brought to a standstill, more detailed reorganization takes place. Some tanks or self-propelled guns are retained, but the majority return to pre-arranged rallying points. Anti-tank guns, machine-guns, mortars, and defensive stores are brought up rapidly, and minefields are laid across the most likely approaches for enemy counter-attacks. Electrically controlled mines are laid over areas through which own tanks may have to advance.

During the advance through the enemy position, special anti-tank groups follow in rear of the assault waves, composed of anti-tank guns, self-propelled guns, and engineers armed with flame-throwers. Their task is to block any frontal counter-attack, while tanks engage the enemy from the flanks.

Artillery fire plan.

5. Fire support is arranged with a view to carrying out the following tasks:—
   (a) Neutralization of rear enemy positions, observation posts, tactical headquarters, and of hostile batteries still firing.
   (b) Destruction of enemy strong points, anti-tank guns, and machine-guns, in the area through which own troops are advancing.
   (c) Repelling enemy counter-attacks, and harassing enemy reserves.

6. The fire plan for the attack consists of a creeping barrage, a series of concentrations, or a combination of both. Normally a creeping barrage is laid down in front of the advancing troops, the first lift being when troops are 100 to 150 yards from the enemy forward defended areas. The barrage subsequently moves forward by lifts of 50 to 100 yards, at a speed allowing for infantry advancing at 50 to 100 yards a minute, according to circumstances, for up to 2,500 yards; after which the advance is supported by planned concentrations, and by observation. A proportion of the artillery is superimposed in depth for the barrage, and some is allotted for destructive shoots on specific points, and for counter-battery fire.

Smoke screens are sometimes used as a means of flank protection, and may also be laid by chemical units.

Immediately the assault begins, some of the artillery move forward to advanced positions so as to support infantry in the depth of the enemy defences. Artillery observation parties accompany battalion and company commanders throughout the operation.

7. Infantry mortars engage enemy forward areas until the attack is launched, when 82-mm mortars go forward with their units. 120-mm. mortars continue to support the attack until the forward areas have been captured, when a proportion move up to come under command of battalions; the remainder are called up when required.

Machine-guns of both the first and second infantry waves support the attack, with particular attention to flank protection. After the capture of the forward areas, they are moved forward and subordinated to companies.

SECTION 15—NIGHT ATTACK

1. The Russians are particularly proud of their skill in conducting night operations; during the war, numerous night attacks supported by tanks were made, culminating in advances of five to ten miles before daybreak.

Preparations for night attacks are made in considerable detail, and troops are brought up to the start line by guides, or follow tapes, or lines of markers with lanterns shining away from the enemy.

The attack is launched at a time when the enemy least expects it, or is least ready to repel it; for example, after a quiet period, the attack might be launched at 0200 hours, but after a hard days fighting at 2300 hours, when tired troops would have just gone to sleep. Apart from consideration of surprise, a favourite time for beginning the attack is two or three hours before dawn, which permits success to be exploited in daylight.

2. In the battle for Berlin, the defence was dazzled by searchlights shining from the flanks and rear of the attackers, a device that was also used during the crossing of the Oder.

Infantry keep at elbow distance from one another, and maintain touch with their tanks, which may be equipped with searchlights. No superfluous troops are employed, but a superiority of three to one over the enemy is considered sufficient for success.

Commanders move close to their units, and maintain communication by wireless, liaison officers, messengers, and light signals. In general, tactics are similar to those employed by day, and the leading wave continues the advance without waiting to mop up.

The attack may be supported by fire, or may be silent.

Air strikes may be used to neutralize enemy artillery, and occasionally to illuminate enemy positions.

SECTION 16—PURSUIT

1. Plans for pursuit are completed in detail either before or during the attack, and pursuit is taken up independently by units as soon as the enemy begins to break. It is maintained with determination, some portions of the pursuing units always maintaining pressure and harassing the withdrawal, while others rest and refuel.

Every effort is made to cut off the enemy retreat, and to this end armoured and mechanized units form the spearhead of the pursuit. When possible, enemy rearguards are by-passed, and then their way of retreat is blocked by obstacles and demolitions arranged by engineers accompanying the leading elements of the pursuit. Parallel pursuit is carried out wherever possible, as it has the advantage of unobstructed advance, combined with the opportunity of harassing the enemy's flank, and cutting withdrawing columns into isolated groups.

2. Long range artillery is employed to bring down harassing fire on cross roads and defiles, with the object of delaying withdrawal, and the arrival of reinforcements.

The air force carries out similar tasks, reconnoitres for advancing enemy reinforcements, and protects the pursuit from air attack.

When hastily constructed defences are encountered, the attack is launched from the line of march.

SECTION 17—AIR SUPPORT IN THE OFFENSIVE

The Soviet Air Force contains a very large proportion of aircraft designed for close support. These appeared in great numbers over the battle-field, holding their own against the Luftwaffe by sheer weight of numbers, in spite of their considerable inferiority in performance.

Each front usually had one air army attached for operations. An air army consisted of about 800 aircraft, made up as follows:—

(a) One fighter corps, of two fighter divisions, each of three fighter regiments, each containing 40 aircraft at full strength.

(b) One ground attack corps, consisting of two ground attack divisions, and one fighter division, similarly organized.

(c) One medium bomber corps, of two divisions, each of three regiments, each containing 32 medium bombers.

Air support for a major assault was usually provided by five or six formations of ground attack aircraft, each consisting of 30 to 36 aircraft, at intervals of 10 to 15 minutes. Fighter escort was nearly always provided. During the artillery preparation, ground attack aircraft were mainly employed in attacking and neutralizing such targets as were beyond artillery range, or invisible to ground observers. A concentrated air attack was normally made on enemy defended areas and gun positions immediately prior to the assault.

After an air strike, some aircraft used to remain over the battle-field until covering aircraft arrived; the latter then remained continuously over the attacking troops ready to engage targets at call from air liaison officers with ground units.

Attacking aircraft report progress of the attack, and information about the enemy; every basic division has an air liaison flight for obtaining additional information, and passing messages.

Medium bombers of air armies were employed almost exclusively for tactical bombing. Operations were nearly always carried out by day, with fighter escort, and were frequently carried out by formations of 40 to 50 medium bombers, flying in groups of nine aircraft. Bombing was usually carried out by flights of three aircraft; targets in the battle area were bombed from heights of 2,500 to 6,000 feet, and those in the rear areas from heights of 10,000 to 16,000 feet.

Air strikes were called for through air liaison officers with ground formations, and advanced airfields were constructed well forward, to provide speedy support.

CHAPTER 6

TACTICS—DEFENCE AND WITHDRAWAL

SECTION 18—GENERAL

1. Soviet policy for defence stresses the importance of depth, and mutually supporting areas sited for all-round defence. Infantry fight with great stubbornness and counter attack whenever possible. The high command exploit this characteristic, and only reinforce a threatened sector when it becomes absolutely essential to do so, in order to prevent a strategic breach; they rely on the infantry to contend every inch of the ground during a withdrawal, until the enemy has committed all his reserves, lengthened and strained his lines of communication. Then, when his supplies are short, and his troops weary, strong armoured counter offensives are launched from either side of the salient, with the object of destroying the enemy spearhead. The battle of Stalingrad, and the Soviet counter-offensives in Pomerania and Hungary in 1945 are typical examples of these tactics.

Planning and layout.

2. Planning of a defensive position is co-ordinated at front or army level, and the general line is fixed on the ground by the front or army commander. Particular attention is paid to natural obstacles, and favourable positions for counter-attack.

Anti-tank defence is considered in conjunction with the defensive layout, but the anti-tank layout is superimposed over it. This is explained further in the section on anti-tank defence.

SECTION 19—ARMY DEFENSIVE AREA

3. An army defensive area is divided into four zones, as follows:—
   Security zone—including battle outposts.
   Main defensive zone.
   Second defensive zone.
   Third defensive zone.

The security zone.

4. This zone stretches to a distance of six to 10 miles forward of the main defensive zone, and contains a series of previously prepared positions and obstacles. Its object is to hold up an attacking enemy, tire him, and gain time for improving the main defence; army reserve units are normally detailed to man this zone, and fight a series of rearguard actions, finally withdrawing through the battle outposts of the main defensive zone. The security zone may be dispensed with if the main defensive zone is already prepared.

Battle outposts.

5. Battle outposts are sited 1,000 to 2,000 yards forward of the main defensive zone to impede surprise enemy thrusts, to deny the enemy ground reconnaissance facilities and artillery observation posts, and to force him to deploy early.

The main defensive zone.

6. This is the most important zone of the defence, and is usually sited behind a natural obstacle; its object is to halt an enemy attack, and it is usually manned by rifle divisions. Depth is approximately 6,000 yards, and alternative positions are prepared immediately in rear, for occupation in case of a withdrawal, or for occupation by a reserve division.

Care is taken to ensure that the forward edge is not too obvious on the ground, and a dummy forward edge is sometimes prepared.

The second defensive zone.

7. The second defensive zone begins 10,000 to 12,000 yards in rear of the front of the main defensive zone. It is occupied by army reserves of infantry, artillery, and anti-tank guns, with the task of counter-attacking enemy formations which succeed in breaking through the main defensive zone. Its depth is approximately 6,000 yards.

The third defensive zone.

8. The third defensive zone is sited 10,000 to 15,000 yards in rear of the front of the second defensive zone. It is the responsibility of the army commander, but is manned by front reserves, with the task of counter attacking enemy forces which break through the second defensive zone.

Army tank reserves are usually sited in this area, out of range of enemy artillery.

Obstacles.

9. Mines are usually laid in large numbers, but in a stereotyped manner. During a counter offensive in 1945, the Germans cleared 80,000 mines from an area 12 miles wide by 10 miles deep.

Forward of the main defensive zone, mining is usually confined to tank approaches, sunken roads, defiles, cross roads, and road blocks. A fairly continuous belt of anti-tank minefields is laid along the front of the main defensive zone, 400 yards in depth.

Inside the main defensive zone, priority is given to mining approaches to the artillery, anti-tank, and divisional reserve areas. Additional mine laying is carried out during lulls in the battle, under fire if necessary.

Other obstacles are planned in conjunction with minefields, and include anti-tank ditches and wire.

SECTION 20—DEPLOYMENT OF A RIFLE DIVISION

1. In all the examples available, Soviet policy for deploying a rifle division and its supporting arms in static defence appears to be mainly line for infantry, and depth for artillery. In the main defensive zone, rifle divisions are deployed in line, with their regiments and battalions in line, though companies and platoons are sited two forward and one back, and some sort of divisional reserve is always constituted. This reserve will normally consist of the majority of the medium tank SP regiment and the motor-cycle reconnaissance battalion. Depth appears to be provided mainly by the army second and third defensive zones, but there is always the proviso that the space between the main and second defensive zones may be filled by a reserve rifle division. A diagram of a rifle division deployed for static defence is at Appendix U.

2. Frontages and depths of units are approximately as follows:—

	Frontage (yards)	Depth (yards)
Rifle division	10,000	5–6,000
Rifle regiment	5,000	2,000
Rifle battalion	2,000	1,500
Rifle company	700	400

3. The Soviet soldier digs himself in very quickly, and conceals his position with considerable skill. Positions consist of a number of one or two-man fox-holes, inter-supporting, and sufficiently deep to enable a man to stand, with the soil removed. As soon as possible, the system is developed into a system of platoon posts, joined by communication trenches.

The sections of rifle platoons are not sited in depth, but in line, in order to make the best use of their weapons frontally. Platoons are sited with two forward, and the third 150 to 300 yards in rear; companies are similarly sited, with 400 to 800 yards between the rear platoons of the two forward companies, and the forward platoons of the reserve company.

SECTION 21—ANTI-TANK DEFENCE

1. Anti-tank defence is planned and co-ordinated on an army level, but divisional commanders are responsible for the anti-tank defence of their own areas. Rifle divisions are often reinforced by an army anti-tank regiment, and some army artillery.

Companies and battalions in areas vulnerable to tank attack are reinforced by divisional anti-tank weapons, and usually concentrate their anti-tank weapons to defend one specific portion of their defensive areas, forming anti-tank areas.

2. The divisional artillery is sited in rear of the infantry defensive areas, and has a secondary anti-tank role. The divisional mobile reserve

of anti-tank weapons is sited in rear of the divisional artillery, and may be augmented by an army anti-tank regiment.

Some tanks and self-propelled guns are allotted to battalions, but the majority are concentrated in rear as a mobile reserve for counter-attack.

3. Anti-tank guns in battalion areas are normally sited in depth, defiladed from the front, with an interval of 200 yards between guns. They are mutually supporting, and cover all gaps between battalion and company areas. Some guns are sited sufficiently far forward as to be able to destroy tanks within 300 to 400 yards of the front line. Tanks and self-propelled guns are usually sited to give depth to company and battalion areas. Rifle units were until recently equipped with anti-tank rifles.

4. The army, or corps, anti-tank regiment, when allotted, is sited in the divisional reserve area, but has several prepared alternative positions sited to meet enemy penetrations. It is usually deployed to form an anti-tank strong point, consisting of mutually supporting troop areas, sited in depth. Guns in troops are sited in diamond formation with 200 yards between guns.

Anti-tank role of divisional artillery.

5. All divisional artillery can engage tanks by direct fire, and have in addition the following anti-tank tasks:—

  (a) Long range concentrations.
  (b) Concentrations on tank assembly areas and start lines.
  (c) Creeping barrages.
  (d) Fixed barrages.

6. Long range concentrations are put down on approaching tank formations, with the object of causing them to disperse, delaying their advance and inflicting casualties. Suitable targets would be defiles, bridges, and fords.

All artillery and mortars are used for concentrations on tank assembly areas and start lines, with similar objects. They are also used for creeping barrages, previously worked out to cover probable enemy attack routes from the start line up to the forward edge of the infantry defences. The purpose of these barrages is to separate tanks from their escorting infantry.

When the attack reaches the forward defended areas, the barrage may remain fixed on the last line, to prevent reinforcements from coming up.

Creeping barrages begin as soon as leading enemy tanks enter the prescribed area.

Anti-tank role of divisional tank self-propelled gun regiments.

7. Some tanks and self-propelled guns are sited to reinforce infantry localities, and dug in to form armoured anti-tank gun or machine-gun posts.

Others are dug in on the flanks of probable tank penetrations, with the object of engaging the enemy from the flanks once he is well within the main defensive zone, and has been stopped frontally by the anti-tank reserves.

SECTION 22—RESERVES AND COUNTER-ATTACK

1. The object of the defence is to break up the attacking formation, separate tanks from their escorting infantry, and then destroy the enemy with previously planned counter-attacks as soon as the attack loses momentum. Commanders always keep a reserve in hand for this purpose, consisting mainly of the divisional tank self-propelled gun regiment, with infantry support. Fire positions are dug for tanks to occupy across the paths of probable penetrations.

Fire support for counter-attacks is given by all available artillery and mortars, including army artillery.

SECTION 23—ARTILLERY SUPPORT

1. As in the attack, major artillery formations may be concentrated behind certain sectors for defence, consisting of large *ad hoc* groupings suited to the task in hand.

Deployment is always in depth, and every troop has several alternative positions prepared and stocked with ammunition.

2. Artillery tasks include:—

(a) Defensive fire tasks in a fairly continuous belt 400 yards deep along the front of the main defensive area.
(b) Harassing fire on possible concentration areas and defiles.
(c) Support of outposts.
(d) Counter battery fire.
(e) Concentrations on forming up points.
(f) Creeping and fixed barrages on attacking formations.
(g) Fire support for counter attacks.
(h) Engagement of tanks by direct fire.

3. Rifle battalions possess their own mortars and machine guns, which are co-ordinated into the defensive fire plan. All mortars and machine guns have several alternative positions.

SECTION 24—ANTI-AIRCRAFT DEFENCE

1. The Soviet Army is not well equipped with heavy anti-aircraft weapons or fire control instruments, but all the basic divisions have light anti-aircraft units armed with 37-mm guns, and anti-aircraft machine guns.

Light anti-aircraft guns are deployed in troops 1,000 to 2,000 yards behind the front of the main defensive zone, with 1,000 to 2,000 yards between troops and 30 yards between guns.

Anti-aircraft divisions, consisting of light and heavy anti-aircraft guns are normally available only for the defence of vital rear installations; an anti-aircraft division can cover an area 10,000 yards wide by 7,000 yards deep.

All anti-aircraft artillery has a secondary anti-tank role, and has alternate positions dug to suit this role.

SECTION 25—AIR SUPPORT IN DEFENCE

1. In defence, the air force carries out the following tasks:—
  (a) Reconnaissance to discover enemy dispositions, and to obtain early warning of the direction and strength of attacks.
  (b) Indication of targets to the artillery.
  (c) Attacks on enemy concentrations.
  (d) Air strikes immediately forward of the main defensive line, called down by air liaison officers with forward rifle units.
  (e) Support of counter attacks in accordance with directions from air liaison officers.

Steady pressure is usually maintained on the enemy by formations of four to 20 aircraft, attacking at frequent intervals. Attacks on the enemy's forward areas are normally carried out by small formations of four to 12 aircraft, operating beyond the range of own artillery. Enemy airfields were attacked by formations of 18 to 36 aircraft, sometimes followed by other similar waves.

SECTION 26—SUMMARY OF DEFENCES

1. An attack on a typical position defended by a Soviet rifle division and supporting arms would encounter the following resistance, in chronological order.
  (a) Concentrations of artillery fire and air strikes while traversing defiles approximately 8,000 yards from the Russian main defences.
  (b) Air strikes, with artillery and mortar concentrations, on forming up places, about 4,000 yards from the main defences.
  (c) Creeping barrages from these areas up to a distance of 200 yards from the main defences.
  (d) Artillery defensive fire together with machine gun and small arms fire.
  (e) A belt of anti-tank gun fire beginning 400 yards from the beginning of the main defences.
  (f) Minefields beginning 400 yards before reaching the infantry localities.

(g) Infantry localities reaching to a depth of 2,000 yards, with a density of at least eight anti-tank or self-propelled guns to 1,000 yards, probably reinforced by dug in tanks.

(h) Minefields 2,000 yards in rear of the forward edge of the infantry localities.

(j) The divisional artillery area, with an average of 8 guns to 1,000 yards, but probably reinforced at the point of penetration by an army anti-tank regiment with a fire frontage of 4,000 yards, a fire depth of the same distance, and a density of 10 guns to 1,000 yards.

(k) Counter attack by 50 medium tanks and 16 medium self-propelled guns, supported by infantry, artillery, and aircraft.

(l) The divisional alternative position.

2. Soviet anti-tank guns normally hold their fire as long as possible before opening fire, and seldom fire at ranges greater than 400 yards.

They expect to destroy at least one tank each before being put out of action; the first Ukrainian front average was two German tanks for each anti-tank gun destroyed.

When the gun is out of action, the detachment fight on as infantry, and are armed for this purpose with rifles and sub-machine guns.

SECTION 27—TANK AND MECHANIZED DIVISIONS IN DEFENCE

1. Tank and mechanized divisions are usually held as front reserve, but can be used either to hold a portion of the defences themselves, or in conjunction with rifle formations. In the former case, they are usually sited across the probable path of the enemy main tank assault, and the general defensive plan is based on similar principles to that of the rifle division. In view of this, it is proposed to study only a medium tank battalion of a tank division with supporting arms occupying a defensive area.

2. The medium tank battalion is usually reinforced by a company of infantry, some anti-tank guns, and some engineers, either from regimental headquarters, the motorized rifle battalion of the medium tank regiment, or from the motorized rifle regiment of the tank division. Heavy tanks and self-propelled guns may be allotted in addition, though the heavy tank self-propelled gun regiment will normally occupy a position in depth as the divisional commanders reserve.

3. Medium tanks are dug in, as fixed machine-gun and anti-tank gun posts, which form the basis of the defensive fire system. Some may be employed as ambushes, or held in battalion mobile reserve. Heavy tanks and self-propelled guns are employed in the latter two roles.

Riflemen are used for outpost duty, and for protection of tanks against enemy infantry. They also engage infantry following behind, or riding on, tanks.

Anti-tank guns are sited to cover defiles, for strengthening outposts, and for ambushes in open ground.

Engineers erect obstacles, clear fields of fire, prepare counter-attack routes, and equip the battalion commander's command post.

Deployment.

4. Outposts are composed of riflemen, reinforced by mortars and anti-tank guns. Some tanks are usually allotted from the battalion commander's reserve to support them and cover their withdrawal.

The two company defended areas are sited in depth for all round defence, and are composed of mutually supporting troop posts, at approximately 200 yards interval. Tanks are usually sited in depth with 100 to 200 yards between tanks; each tank has a previously prepared alternative position dug ready for it, with a covered connecting route. These alternative positions are occupied in order to fulfil alternative tasks, or to avoid destruction.

A battalion reserve is sited in depth with the tasks of preventing enemy outflanking movements, supporting company areas with counter attacks, and destruction of enemy penetrating the defended area.

A diagram of a tank battalion area in defence is at Appendix V. The battalion is on the old establishment of two companies in place of three.

SECTION 28—WITHDRAWAL

1. Withdrawal may only be carried out after permission has been obtained from the front commander in the case of an army, and from the army commander in the case of a division. When it has been decided that a withdrawal is necessary, routes are prepared, and anti-aircraft protection is allotted to defiles and vulnerable areas.

Rearguards normally consist of motorized infantry reinforced with anti-tank guns, anti-aircraft guns, and tanks. Particular attention is paid to the choice of rear guard commanders, who are picked for their staunchness; seniority is no criterion.

An extensive demolition plan is prepared on an army level, specifying priorities and times.

The first units to be withdrawn are the army artillery, and the supply echelons, who move back under cover of darkness one or two days before the main withdrawal. The main forces then disengage themselves, usually on a broad front in darkness or under cover of artillery fire and smoke. On occasions, withdrawal follows immediately after a counter attack.

2. Rearguards are formed either from army troops or from divisional reserves; they occupy positions in rear of the main defences, and the main forces withdraw through them. The rearguard then withdraws by tactical bounds, on a timed programme. Destruction of bridges is the responsibility of the rearguard commander, who also sends detachments to block side roads, and parallel routes.

Rearguard tactics include counter attacks with limited objectives, usually carried out by tanks, supported by infantry, artillery, and aircraft. The air force endeavours to delay the enemy by attacking his forward elements.

Communications are mainly by wireless or by liaison officers.

CHAPTER 7

TACTICS—SPECIAL CONDITIONS

SECTION 29—FIGHTING IN BUILT-UP AREAS

Attack.

1. The first phase of a battle for a town consists of driving in outposts, and surrounding the built-up area completely. Some portions of the attacking force are given the task of preventing enemy counter attacks from interfering with the battle for the town, while others carry out the assault.

The town is then divided into areas, which are allotted to regiments or battalions. The attack is launched from several different directions at once, after artillery and air preparation, and is supported by artillery fire and air strikes. The battle then takes the form of a number of independent actions by small units, who infiltrate into the town, attacking one block of buildings after another, consolidating their gains, and clearing all houses, tunnels, and sewers as they advance.

Shock groups are formed to deal with individual strong points; all personnel carry anti-personnel and anti-tank grenades, and groups are reinforced by engineers with demolition charges, flame-throwers, self-propelled guns, and tanks.

Other tanks cover all exits from the town, and a tank reserve is held to engage enemy counter attacks.

Consolidation of captured buildings is carried out with engineer assistance, and captured streets are blocked by obstacles.

Defence.

2. The general principles of defence apply to defence of a town. Withdrawal can only be sanctioned by the senior officer present, and commanders of garrisons are specially picked.

Positions are sited in depth. When time is needed for development of the position, troops man a security zone, and withdraw slowly on to the main defensive zone, which usually overlaps the town itself. The town is organized for defence in depth, and districts are allotted to units. Groups of buildings at cross roads and squares are transformed into mutually supporting groups of strong points, and every house in these groups is organized for story defence. Ground floors and cellars are prepared so that the garrison can fire along streets, and upper floors so as to fire down on to streets, or engage neighbouring buildings and courtyards. Adequate stocks of supplies are dumped in every strong point.

Solid buildings are connected by holes made through the walls, which are reinforced with sandbags and additional brickwork, roofs are strengthened by beams, earth, and by pulling down the upper stories.

Cellars are also connected, and used for intercommunication. Other means are sewers, underground railways, and communication trenches dug across streets.

Streets are mined and blocked with any available material, such as tramcars or vehicles.

Artillery support is usually provided by single guns firing direct from strongpoints, but sometimes an artillery group outside the town provides fire at call from FOOs with the garrison.

Single tanks and self-propelled guns can also be sited in strong points but armour is normally kept in reserve for counter attack.

SECTION 30—WINTER WARFARE

1. Factors affecting operations in Northern Russia which arise in winter and not in summer are cold, deep snow, and short days. The Soviet Army was better able to cope with these conditions than were the Germans, and therefore always held the initiative during winter.

2. Cold is counteracted by the following methods:—
   (a) Keeping troops under shelter as much as possible. Positions are based on inhabited localities or woods, and bivouac tents or improvised shelters are used whenever troops occupy temporary positions.
   (b) Strongpoints and pill boxes are heated by stoves, and attacking troops are brought from their improvised shelters in the assembly areas up to their start lines at the last moment, normally just before dawn.
   (c) Tanks, vehicles, and guns are enclosed as much as possible with snow walls and branches, and stoves are issued for heating.
   (d) Special clothing is issued to troops, particularly to ski-troops.
   (e) Warming posts are established all along lines of communication, and in rest areas, where drivers can break their journey to warm themselves.
   (f) Ice or snow is melted and filtered under engineer arrangements.
   (g) Casualty clearing stations are sited well forward, so that wounded can be treated before they freeze to death.

3. The depth of snow interferes with mobility. The Soviet Army consider that only tanks with special snow tracks, and infantry on skis, can operate in two feet of snow, and that three feet is the upper limit for any movement. In view of this, the Soviet Army makes extensive

use of ski troops, dressed in white clothing for concealment; their role is to reconnoitre, protect flanks, carry out encircling movements, and harass the enemy rear.

All units improvise sledges for machine guns, mortars, and for carrying stores; artillery is fitted with runners, and tractors may have spikes fitted to their tracks.

Before an assault, trenches are cleared of snow, and are extended as close as possible to the enemy positions, and sometimes, so as to encircle them. Attacking troops run along these trenches, and only leave them at the last moment. Tanks accompany infantry in support, but over routes carefully reconnoitred, to ensure that they do not have to cross deep snow drifts in undulating ground.

Paths are developed into roads, and kept clear, either by troops in reserve, or by conscription of local labour. Liaison personnel are all trained to use skis.

Owing to the shortness of hours of daylight, troops operate to a large extent by night. The Russians often use small bodies of troops to carry out important operations. If they become too heavily involved, they can normally hold out until dusk, when they can make their escape.

SECTION 31—RIVER CROSSING

1. The Soviet Army has had considerable experience in assault crossings of rivers of all types.

The principles for a successful assault crossing are:—
(a) Thorough reconnaissance.
(b) Careful planning.
(c) Concentration of superior forces, and sufficient fire power to neutralize enemy defensive fire.
(d) Surprise.
(e) Speed of assault and consolidation.
(f) Simultaneous crossings at different points on a wide front.
(g) Diversionary crossings on lines of advance of secondary importance, but of primary importance to the enemy, to distract his attention from the main thrust, and to induce him to move reserves to the area of the diversionary crossing.
(h) Dummy crossings.
(j) Concealment of preparation for the assault.
(k) Good organization of anti-aircraft, anti-tank, and anti-chemical warfare defences in the crossing areas.
(l) Timely and skilful handling of crossing equipment, standard and improvised.

2. Once the assault has been begun, every effort is made to carry it through to its conclusion; if it finally fails, no further attempts are made in that area, and the main thrust is shifted to an area where the operation has been more successful.

3. During an advance to contact, or a pursuit, armoured and motorized units are sent on ahead of the main forces to seize bridgeheads, supported by artillery and aircraft. Airborne units may be used.

If the leading units fail to capture bridgeheads, then a quick assault crossing is organized by the corps, divisional, or, at the lowest level, regimental commander; preparation for such an operation is limited to two days.

If the quick assault fails, forces are regrouped, and a large scale operation, involving considerable preparation, is mounted by the army commander.

4. Crossings are carried out:—
    (a) By day, with artillery and air preparation and support.
    (b) At dusk, with artillery and air preparation; by this method the main forces cross under cover of darkness.
    (c) Before dawn, either silent for deception, or with artillery and air support.

Assembly.

5. (a) Formations and units are concentrated at the following distances from the river.
    Army formations . . . . 15 to 20 miles.
    Army Second echelon divisions . . . 4 to 8 miles.
    Army First echelon divisions . . . . 2½ to 4 miles.
    (b) Formations and units are detailed to assault waves and crossing places in waiting areas, two miles from the river. From there they move up to starting areas, by battalion groups, 1,000 to 2,000 yards from the river.
    (c) Flights prepare for their crossing at start lines, 100 to 200 yards from the water's edge.
    (d) Assault crossing equipment is concentrated as near the river as possible.
    (e) All concentration areas are concealed as far as possible from enemy air and ground observation.

Methods of crossing.

6. A rifle regiment normally carries out an assault crossing on a frontage of 1,000 to 1,500 yards, with at least two crossing places; a rifle division crosses on a frontage of 2 to 2½ miles, with not less than four.

7. Crossings may be of the following types:—
    (a) *Swim crossings:*—For rifle units using improvised floats and rafts over narrow rivers. One crossing is a place where a company can cross on one flight.
    (b) *Ford crossings:*—Areas which can be crossed without special equipment.
    (c) *Landing craft crossings:*—For rifle, cavalry, and even armoured formations, if powerful landing craft are available. Crossings are chosen to take one company in a flight.

(d) *Ferry crossings:*—For artillery, tanks, and vehicles. Each ferry point consists of one to three ferries, with varying capacities.

(e) *Bridge crossings:*—Either at an existing bridge, or from standard bridging equipment. Normal load capacities are six, 10, 16, 30, and 60 tons.

8. By day, or at dusk, crossings are carried out in the following order:—

(a) Forward infantry sub-units, comprising sub-machine gunners, reconnaissance parties, anti-tank guns, and sappers. The crossing is carried out during or after artillery and air preparation, and supported by all available fire power. Their object is to secure the crossing of the first wave, by destroying undamaged enemy strong points, clearing lanes between obstacles, and organizing anti-tank defence.

(b) The first wave follows, on a broad front, with the object of securing the crossing and deployment of subsequent waves and the main forces, by capturing and consolidating a bridgehead.

The first wave normally consists of a battalion for a regimental, and two to four battalions for a divisional crossing. In addition, where the requisite crossing equipment is available, the first wave contains tanks, self-propelled guns, anti-tank guns, sappers, FOOs, and infantry signals detachments.

(c) The main forces, in a series of waves. Artillery and mortars cross in waves, so that a large proportion is always in position on one bank or the other to provide fire support.

9. By night, the whole of the first wave crosses at once, on a broad front, in order to achieve surprise; no sub-units are sent in advance.

10. When the width of the river exceeds 100 yards, the crossing usually begins during the artillery and air preparation period.

11. In one example, where the width of the river was 65 yards, a rifle division crossed by means of two landing craft crossings, one cable ferry, and one pontoon bridge in 6½ hours. The bridge was completed four hours after the assault began. A regiment with supporting arms, using one landing craft crossing and the cable ferry took four hours, and a battalion crossed in landing craft in four flights, taking two hours.

SECTION 32—PARTISAN WARFARE

1. The Russians made effective use of partisans to disorganize the German lines of communication, and obtain information about the enemy. Immediately after enemy occupation in 1941, partisan resistance was carried out by small bands of civilians, together with a few soldiers who had lost their units during the retreat, under the direction of local members of the Communist Party. They hid in forests or swamps, and carried out small unco-ordinated raids on the enemy lines of communication.

In 1942, leaders of partisan bands were summoned to Moscow, where they were trained for partisan warfare, and briefed for future policy. Then, together with military and political assistants, they were sent back to their units, with orders to recruit large numbers of partisans and carry out large scale operations behind the enemy lines.

They were very successful in raising volunteers, to such an extent that the partisan strength at its highest reached a total of over 200,000 despite the fact that the Germans claim to have killed 130,000. Partisan bands usually operated in brigades approximately 3,000 strong, occasionally strengthed with a few guns. They were under military discipline, defection and cowardice being punished by death.

2. Partisan operations were planned and controlled by a political headquarters in Moscow, through regional and district committees in occupied territory, who in their turn controlled local committees and partisan bands. Partisan staffs were attached to fronts for liaison purposes, to co-ordinate partisan activities with future operations of the Red Army.

Administration was carried out by air supply, either by parachute dropping or by air landing. In the latter case, wounded and families were evacuated to Moscow on the return journey. Air supply reached its maximum in May 1943, when 3,300 sorties were flown.

For food, partisans normally relied upon local produce, of which there was sufficient for their needs. Other necessities were obtained by raids on enemy dumps.

3. The partisan threat became serious toward the end of 1942, and the Germans were compelled to employ forces of regular troops up to 30,000 strong to control their activities. The most effective method was to surround a band, and then close in and annihilate it.

One typical partisan band was formed in December 1941, consisting of only 30 men; strength increased to 500 in June 1942, and remained steady until December, as the influx of recruits was offset by 350 casualties, the majority through sickness. In the summer of 1943, many more recruits joined the band, probably due to the successes of the Red Army, and the strength increased to over 2,000. The band was surrounded and liquidated by strong German forces in October 1943; captured documents claimed the following successes up to January 1943:—

Germans killed	4,631
Collaborators killed	248
Trains derailed and destroyed	55
Bridges blown	128
Own losses, killed	52

4. Partisans also supplied military intelligence for the Red Army; in order that a co-ordinated picture might be obtained they were issued with a comprehensive questionnaire from Moscow. Agents were recruited from the civil population, and from Soviet citizens in German

employ, either voluntarily, or under compulsion, by threats against the individual and his, or her, relatives. Women who could be persuaded to form friendships with German personnel were the best source of information.

Intelligence was normally collated and checked by partisan brigade, or equivalent, headquarters, and passed on by courier, or by wireless in cipher.

5. Partisans were also employed in spreading Soviet propaganda, with notable success against the German propaganda organization. Field printing presses were issued from Moscow, and even cinema-projectors, the current for which was supplied by hand-operated dynamos. Propaganda meetings and film shows were held in villages not garrisoned by the Germans.

CHAPTER 8

AIRBORNE OPERATIONS

SECTION 33—GENERAL

1. The Soviet Army has practically no experience in carrying out large scale airborne operations. In 1943, two airborne brigades took part in an operation intended to assist ground forces in crossing the Dneiper, but were annihilated, and the operation was a complete failure. German sources state that troops were too lightly armed, and that pilots were not sufficiently trained in co-operation with parachutists.

Airborne forces were also used in 1945 to occupy key points in Manchuria and Korea, but were not severely tested for efficiency, owing to the lack of opposition.

2. Soviet Army airborne troops are a special branch of the service, directly subordinated to the Ministry of Armed Forces. They consist of parachute, air-landing (glider), and air-transported units, and are allotted by the High Command to commanders of fronts or armies; for specific operations, however, they may be placed directly under the commander of airborne troops.

3. Tasks of airborne troops are as follows:—
(a) To support ground troops in surrounding and liquidating the enemy.
(b) To disorganize control and administration in the enemy rear areas.
(c) To occupy and hold important defiles and sectors in the enemy rear.
(d) To occupy or destroy enemy airfields and air bases.
(e) To secure disembarkation of seaborne troops by seizing coastal areas.

4. Airborne troops have both tactical and strategic roles.

Tactical Role.

5. In a tactical role, airborne troops are used in brigade, battalion, or company strength with only light supporting arms to accomplish tactical tasks in direct co-operation with the ground forces. Their tasks include disrupting the enemy rear, preventing enemy reserves from moving up to the battle-field, encircling enemy groups in the battle area, destroying communications, hindering staff work, and destruction of supplies. Their objectives would include:—

- (a) Artillery positions.
- (b) Staffs and headquarters.
- (c) Tactical reserves (sometimes).
- (d) Stores and transport.
- (e) Crossings, defiles and dominating heights, on the enemy lines of communication.
- (f) Signal centres.
- (g) Isolated enemy rear positions.
- (h) Bridgeheads for assault crossings over water obstacles.

6. During the advance to contact, airborne troops are initially employed to forestall the enemy in occupation of points suitable to cover deployment of the main forces. Subsequently they are used as shown in para 5 above.

7. In defence, airborne troops are used to a limited extent to disorganize the enemy rear areas.

Strategic role.

8. Airborne troops in a strategic role are employed in up to corps strength, and are usually reinforced with light tank battalions, anti-tank and field artillery, mortars, and anti-aircraft machine-guns. They also include motorcycle units for reconnaissance, who become ski-troops in winter.

9. In the initial phases of an offensive operation, the main tasks of airborne troops are destruction of road and rail communications, and direct action against transport, to prevent the enemy from moving up reserves, ammunition, and supplies.

During the penetration phase of the attack, airborne troops occupy positions in rear of the enemy defensive zone, to cut off supplies and reinforcements.

In all further phases of the offensive, the main role is support of ground mobile troops; at the culmination of a successful offensive, a fairly large number of airborne troops are dropped on enemy routes of withdrawal, to assist their encirclement and annihilation.

Roles in the advance to contact, and defence, are similar to those of tactical forces.

SECTION 34—PREPARATION AND OPERATION

Reconnaissance.

1. A front's reconnaissance plan always provides for the possibility of airborne landings in the enemy rear; but once it has been decided to launch an airborne operation, more extensive reconnaissance takes place. The first object of reconnaissance is to select suitable landing grounds and dropping zones, and then to reconnoitre for all enemy forces and defences within 50 miles of the area chosen.

Reconnaissance is carried out by means of air observation and photography, espionage, and by parachutists. The latter are briefed verbally, and given the minimum information about forthcoming operations. They are usually landed by night, or at dawn, and communicate with their bases by wireless, carrier pigeon, messages picked up by aircraft, or personally on their return. The latter course is only feasible when it is possible to pick them up by plane.

Other groups of parachutists are often dropped outside the area of proposed operations as a deception measure, care being taken to drop them in areas suitable for landing airborne troops.

Assembly.

2. When time permits, and enemy air activity is not too strong, heavy loads, such as guns, tanks, and vehicles, are loaded before the general assembly and emplaning. The main forming-up points for airborne troops are chosen within a maximum of 1,000 yards from the aircraft, under cover, and with shelters available. Movement to the forming-up points is carried out 1 to 1½ hours before the emplaning is due to begin.

Signals for the various stages of emplaning are often given by rockets.

Flight.

3. The route is chosen so as to avoid enemy anti-aircraft and fighter defences, to reach the objective as soon as possible, and with consideration to secrecy and deception.

Communications during flight are maintained by wireless; messages are passed in plain language, using a coded map.

If the commander of an airborne wave receives information during flight to the effect that the air or ground situation has altered, he may change his landing point, but must report his decision to the commander by wireless.

Landing.

4. Soviet military authorities state that airborne troops can be dropped in any season of the year, and at any time of the day; flight and landing by night is carried out only by small independent waves.

Troops are dropped from minimum safe heights, and supplies immediately after them, from heights of 300 to 600 feet. Load-carrying aircraft normally fly at three to five minutes behind troop-carrying aircraft.

Parachutes are either concealed or destroyed after landing.

Gliders and aircraft are landed once the necessary ground has been secured by paratroops. Airborne light tanks and vehicles may be used to clear damaged aircraft from the runways.

Operation.

5. After landing, airborne troops overcome any local enemy resistance, and then assemble in previously determined areas. Their tactical employment is then centralized, or decentralized. The first airborne wave contains a specially trained detachment, detailed to occupy all telephone, telegraph, and wireless stations in the landing zone, so as to prevent the enemy learning about the landing; and to spread false information.

For centralized action, airborne units maintain touch, and work together as a co-ordinated body for action against enemy formations, for capturing major objectives, and for holding tactically important positions. Small detachments are, however, detached to operate in a harassing role.

Decentralized action is used in large areas to disorganize enemy control and command, to hinder supplies and troop movements, and to destroy small enemy detachments. The force is divided into battalions, companies, platoons, or even sections. which are allotted independent tasks. They all work in accordance with a co-ordinated plan, so that they can switch over to centralized action if necessary; distances between units are approximately as follows:—

Sections and platoons	3,000 to 5,000 yards
Companies	4 to 5 miles
Battalions	6 to 8 miles

As the airborne troops are short of fire support, they make the best use of surprise and the cover of darkness; their regulations particularly stress that they must avoid actions with enemy forces which are not of advantage to the main operation.

If it should be necessary to concentrate troops in another area after an operation, the area chosen is usually uninhabited, covered, and inaccessible to tanks. Companies assemble first, at distances of 1,000 to 2,000 yards from each other, then battalions at distances of two to three miles; brigades are seldom concentrated. Assembly areas are usually chosen at least six to ten miles from the previous area of operations.

Administration.

6. Maintenance is carried out by air, usually by night or at dawn, and supply dumps are established in uninhabited places, under cover. Some technicians accompany the force, equipped to carry out minor

repairs, and troops are trained in the use of captured enemy weapons and vehicles.

Medical aid posts are set up in concealed localities, and wounded are evacuated by air if possible, usually by night. Normally, however, they rely on ground forces advancing and making contact with them, in which case the wounded are evacuated through the land forces organization.

SECTION 35—AIR SUPPORT

1. During preparation for an operation, the air force is responsible for reconnaissance to find out the air and ground strength of the enemy in the area of projected operations. Particular attention is paid to locating enemy armoured or mechanized units within 40 miles of the landing zone. Just before, and during the approach flight, aircraft are sent out to find out weather conditions in the operational area.

Fighter aircraft escort the transport aircraft during the approach flight.

During the landing, fighters protect the landing zone from enemy air attack, engage enemy anti-aircraft positions, give close support to the troops that have landed, engage approaching enemy reserves, and provide smoke screens, if required. Bombers may also be allotted for close support.

After the landing, the fighter aircraft escort transport and bomber planes back to base.

CHAPTER 9

SUPPLY IN THE FIELD

SECTION 36—ADMINISTRATION

1. The underlying principles of supply in the Soviet Army during the war may be summarized as follows:—
   (a) Improvisation, covering ruthless exploitation of local resources, and the manual dexterity of the Russian soldier.
   (b) Exploitation of the frugality of the soldier, who is accustomed to a standard of living well below that of the Western nations.
   (c) Standardization of equipment, facilitating supply of spare parts and ammunition.
   (d) Intensive salvage and use of captured equipment.
   (e) Centralization of supply transport, and pooling of transport in an emergency.

2. Supply depots all over the USSR were organized by the Department of the Chief of Rear Services. Supplies of all types were conveyed from these depots to fronts by rail, where they were unloaded, divided into portions for armies, and despatched to army supply bases by rail.

At army supply bases, bulk was broken, and supplies were divided into separate army field depots as follows:—

Ammunition	Veterinary supplies
Weapons and equipment	Spares for vehicles
POL	Spares for tanks
Provisions	Engineer stores
Medical supplies	Signal stores

3. Supplies were sometimes moved forward from army supply bases to supply railway stations in rifle corps rear areas, each supply railway station serving three rifle divisions; from there they were moved by MT to divisional exchange points, where supplies were received, stored, and issued to regiments.

Divisional MT moved supplies from supply railway stations to divisional exchange points, if the distance was within 25 miles; if more than 25 miles, and less than 100 miles, army and divisional MT combined to move supplies, and if over 100 miles, an advanced army supply base was set up on the boundary of the divisional and army rear areas, 20 miles behind the forward troops. Armies were responsible for transporting supplies to the advanced army supply base.

4. POL was taken direct by army transport to divisional exchange points, where divisional POL points were set up, and units drew their fuel requirements.

Tank formations drew direct from supply railway stations if they were within 60 miles, otherwise they were assisted from army sources.

Divisions carried a total of two refills for every vehicle.

5. Thirteen ration scales were in existence in the Soviet army during the war, the best of which was for the front line soldier, and the lowest for personnel in hospitals.

Fresh vegetables were obtained locally. Other rations were carried as follows:—

In the pack	1 days supply
At the field kitchens of battalions.	1 days supply
By regiments	1 days supply
At the divisional exchange point	2 days supply

6. Ammunition supply was organized by the artillery, who co-ordinated the requirements of rifle regiments. Transport was provided from divisional resources, as required by the artillery commander. When there was an urgent demand, army or divisional transport delivered direct to gun positions and regimental ammunition points.

7. Medical evacuation was based on the principle of higher units evacuating casualties from lower units; the regimental medical company collected from battalion dressing stations, and so on.

All casualties were evacuated beyond army collecting points except for those who were likely to recover very rapidly, and those whom it would have been dangerous to move.

8. Workshops form an integral part of all divisions, and carry out all first and second line repairs; third line repairs are carried out by army workshops.

German sources state that Russian tank recovery was very good.

9. Russian railways can be switched from civil to military control at very short notice, and extensive use is made of both rail and water transport facilities.

Motor transport during the war was allotted approximately as follows:—

Front	one brigade of 1,000 vehicles
Rifle army	two battalions of 400 vehicles each
Rifle division	one company of 100 vehicles

10. The administrative areas of rifle divisions reach for a distance of 20 miles in rear of the combatant units, and those of regiments five to $7\frac{1}{2}$ miles. In attack all lines of supply are shortened as much as possible, as may be seen from the table below:—

		Distance from front line	
	Unit	In attack	In defence
Ammunition supply	Company	500 yards	500 yards
point	Battalion	1 to 2 miles	3 miles
	Regiment	3 to 4 miles	5 to 6 miles
	Division	5 to 6 miles	8 to 9 miles
Rations and POL	Battalion	2 to 3 miles	3 miles
supply point	Regiment	3 to 4 miles	5 to 6 miles
	Division	5 to 6 miles	8 to 9 miles
Medical posts	Company	300 to 500 yards	1000 yards
	Battalion	500 to 1000 yards	2000 yards
	Regiment	1 to 3 miles	$2\frac{1}{2}$ to 3 miles
	Division	4 miles	7 miles
Army mobile field hospital		15 miles	20 miles
Divisional field bakery		12 miles	20 miles
Vehicle collecting	Regiment	5 miles	6 miles
points (for recovery)	Division	8 miles	10 miles

CHAPTER 10

TRAINING AND CONDITIONS OF SERVICE

SECTION 37—TRAINING

Military training outside the Army.

1. Military training in the USSR embraces not only the armed forces, but also school children, and adults in civilian occupations. All Union Voluntary Societies exist for the promotion of aviation, for the promotion of the Army, and for the promotion of the Navy—respectively called DOSAV, DOSARM and DOSFLOT. The creation of these organizations was published in May 1948. They supersede the Osoaviakhim, whose functions were to train the vast mass of civilian population in certain specialist qualifications, such as engineering, shooting, gliding, and chemical warefare, which would be of value to the fighting services in the event of an emergency. The society was of great value during the war, and its three successors can be expected to be co-ordinated more closely with the three services.

Army training.

2. Training within the Soviet Army is influenced by the increased mechanization of all types of formations, the need for close co-operation between all arms, and the building up of airborne formations. These factors can be expected to have a great effect particularly on the training of staffs. It is believed that all staffs down to corps level are being trained in the use of airborne formations.

Military schools and academies of all types exist for the purpose of training officers, NCOs, and officer cadets. The most important of these is the Voroshilov Higher Military Academy, which is attended by senior officers, ranking from army commanders to divisional commanders. Instruction includes tactics on an army and front level, administration, and the handling of all arms.

At the other end of the scale are the Suvorov schools, which train boys to become officer cadets, with an annual output of 7,000. On passing out of Suvorov schools, boys join appropriate officer cadet schools, where they complete their training, and subsequently receive commissions.

Shortage of specialists such as signallers drivers and mechanics, can be expected to influence the training of the Soviet Army for several years to come. Efforts are being made to develop the mechanical instinct in all Soviet troops, without which wastage of material and inefficiency are inevitable.

3. Political training plays an important part in the training programme of every unit. An average programme would include four hours within training hours, and four hours outside them, weekly. Political training is considered particularly important in the Soviet

zones of occupation, since it is in these zones that Russian soldiers are most liable to become politically unsound through contact with other ways of life.

4. Conscripts are normally called up in the autumn under arrangements made by military districts, and are despatched to their units early in December.

Training of all types is carried out in accordance with directives issued through G channels. The winter months are spent in individual training, and unit outdoor exercises begin in April, culminating in corps and army manoeuvres in October and November.

5. Unit training of NCOs is co-ordinated at a high level. Every division has a training battalion attached, which sends its companies out to regiments. The organization of a NCOs training company in a rifle regiment is shown in Appendix D. Training battalions probably have their policy co-ordinated by parent units at Military district headquarters.

The object of these training battalions is to train potential NCOs and specialists for the division. Students who complete a course, which normally lasts for six to nine months, are promoted to anything from serjeant to lance corporal, according to the standard of efficiency attained. It is believed that the training battalions remain attached to divisions in the event of war.

SECTION 38—CONDITIONS OF SERVICE

1. Personnel of the Soviet Army serve in one of the following three categories:—
   (a) As conscripts, who are enlisted as privates, but may become NCOs during their service, which is normally for two years.
   (b) As NCOs or specialists on extended service or deferred demobilization.
   (c) As officers, who serve indefinitely until transferred to the reserve.

After completion of their service as conscripts, NCOs and specialists may volunteer for further service, and if accepted may receive promotion, or an increase in pay. Certain specialists are at present being compulsorily retained for indefinite periods.

2. Officers serve indefinitely, but are transferred to the reserve if they do not rise above certain ranks by certain ages. These age limits are as follows:—

Rank	Age limit
Junior lieutenant	25 years
Lieutenant	30 ,,
Senior lieutenant	35 ,,
Captain	40 ,,
Lieut.-Colonel	50 ,,

An officer with 25 years of active service may request to be put on the retired list, and receives a pension consisting of his full basic pay of rank, but not the extra pay for length of service.

Officers retiring with less than 25 years service are given pensions on a reduced scale.

Pay.

3. Pay consists of three elements, for rank, for appointment, and for length of total service. The rates are as follows:—

Rank	Roubles per month	Appointment	Roubles per month	Probable years service	Roubles per month	TOTAL per month
Major General	1200	Div. comd.	2000	17	400	3600 (£180)
Colonel	1000	Regt. comd.	1500	15	300	2800 (£140)
Major	800	Bn. comd.	1000	10	150	1950 (£98)
Captain	700	Coy. comd.	700	5	70	1470 (£74)
Lieutenant	500	Pl. comd.	650	3	32	1182 (£59)
Sjt. Major	–	Sjt. major	300	6	840	1140 (£57)
Serjeant	–	Serjeant	120	4	500	620 (£31)
Private	30	–	–	3	300	330 (£16)
Private	30	–	–	Less than 3 years	–	30 (£1.10.0)

The pound sterling was worth 21 roubles in the USSR in June 1948.

It must be remembered, however, that the cost of living is very high; Black bread costs two shillings per lb. sugar eight shillings per lb. and a bottle of beer costs 10 shillings.

Marriage allowance is not issued, and disturbance allowance is permissible once only; there are no other allowances. There is no deduction for income tax, but some deductions are made for state loans, party subscriptions, etc.

In the Soviet Air Force, deductions include approximately 15 per cent for flying training, six per cent for being childless; no deductions on the latter count are made for two or more children.

In occupied countries, officers and serjeants may draw a limited amount in local currency, but the remainder is compulsorily transferred to individual accounts inside the USSR.

Other ranks are paid in full in local currency, after similar deductions.

Amenities.

4. Personnel extending their service voluntarily are promised better rations than the conscripts, and in addition receive coupons quarterly, enabling them to buy clothing, toilet articles, and extra cigarettes from the official shop.

Officers receive no free issue of cigarettes, but may purchase a daily ration. Ordinary conscripts receive a few grammes of very low grade loose tobacco per day as part of their ration scale.

Leave.

5. Conscripts get no leave, but officers and personnel on extended service are granted 30 days leave exclusive of travelling time every year. Compassionate leave is sometimes granted to all ranks in the case of the death of a mother, father, or child.

Troops in occupied territory are confined to barracks in their spare time, and are forbidden to have any contact with the local population.

Married quarters are available inside the USSR. Some families were originally permitted to join their husbands in occupied territories, but this privilege has since been withdrawn, and most families have now been repatriated.

CHAPTER 11

EQUIPMENT

SECTION 39—GENERAL

General.

1. Serviceability, achieved through simplicity of design and robust construction, is the chief characteristic of Soviet Army weapons. Although they are frequently of noticeably rough external finish and have seldom embodied any important technical innovation, they are, in general, effective and often impressive specimens of their class.

Armoured Fighting Vehicles.

2. In recent years, the Russians have concentrated on the production of two types of tank, a medium and a heavy, weighing approximately 30 and 50 tons respectively. The two tanks which are at present standard in these weight classes—the T34/85 mounting an 85-mm gun and the Josef-Stalin mounting a 122-mm gun—have been evolved from two basic pre-war designs by an up-gunning and up-armouring process accompanied by progressive sloping of armour and the search for a low silhouette. The Mark 3 Josef-Stalin tank (JS3) is the best example of this development.

The chassis of these two tanks are also used to provide self-propelled mountings for field and anti-tank guns. One other tank chassis is also used in this way; the chassis of the former light tank, production of which was discontinued during the war, is still used in modified form as a self-propelled mounting, notably for the 76·2-mm field gun under the title SU76.

Artillery.

3. The Russians laid great emphasis during the war on the development and production of anti-tank guns. In addition nearly every artillery piece in the field was supplied with armour piercing ammunition.

The weapons which are at present standard in the anti-tank role are the 45-mm Model 42, the 57-mm Model 43, and the 100-mm Model 44. This last equipment marked the peak of Russian wartime anti-tank gun development and is still their most powerful towed anti-tank weapon.

The standard infantry gun is the 76·2-mm Model 43—a lightweight short range equipment.

The standard field artillery gun is the 76·2-mm Model 42. This is the latest in the Soviet series of 3-inch field equipments; it embodies a light-weight carriage and has an important secondary role as an anti-tank gun. Its howitzer counterpart in the divisional artillery is the 122-mm Howitzer Model 38.

The two standard medium artillery weapons are the 122-mm Gun, Model 31/37 and the 152-mm Gun Howitzer, Model 37; both are mounted on the same carriage. Another medium weapon is the 152-mm Howitzer, Model 38 which is being superseded by the 152-mm Howitzer, Model 43. The later equipment consists of the barrel of the 152-mm Howitzer, Model 38 mounted on a slightly modified version of the carriage of the divisional 122-mm Howitzer, Model 38.

The heavy artillery weapons consist of the 152-mm Gun, Model 35, the 203-mm Howitzer, Model 31, and the 280-mm Howitzer, Model 39. These are all mounted on the same tracked carriage. The equipments normally travel in two loads, *ie*, the gun barrel is moved on a separate transporter.

Soviet super-heavy artillery comprises the 210-mm Gun, Model 1940 and the 305-mm Howitzer, Model 1940—both on the same mounting, which consists of two main parts, a box type structure (sunk into the ground during action) and the superstructure. The equipments travel in 3 loads—(a) gun barrel, (b) superstructure and (c) basic structure, each having its special transporter.

Soviet anti-aircraft artillery in the field is chiefly composed of the 25-mm, Model 41 (single and twin equipments), the 37-mm, Model 39, the 76·2-mm, Model 38 and the 85-mm, Model 39. The latter two guns have the same common carriage and the same exterior appearance except that the 85-mm gun is fitted with a muzzle brake.

Field rocket launchers.

4. Multiple rocket launchers were introduced by the Russians early in the war and as a form of auxiliary field artillery won a considerable reputation. The present standard types are normally mounted on wheeled lorry chassis and fire rockets of 8, 13, and 30-cm diameter.

Infantry weapons and Mortars.

5. The Soviet service rifle is the Mossin-Nagant, Model 91/30, with 5-round magazine. Its long spike bayonet attaches to the muzzle. A sniper's version with telescopic sight is made. Two shortened versions known as the Carbine, Model 38 (no bayonet) and Carbine,

Model 44 (with permanently attached folding spike bayonet on the right hand side) are in common use. Self-loading rifles were early introduced (1936): the latest model known is the 7·62-mm Tokarev, Model 40. Machine carbines rapidly sprang into prominence during the war; successive models were produced in 1940, 1941, and 1943 of which the last two are still current.

The standard light machine gun is the 7·62-mm Degtyarev 'DP'. The medium machine gun class comprises the 7·62-mm Maxim, Model 1910 (water cooled) and the 7·62-mm Goryunov, Model 43 (air-cooled). A 12·7-mm machine gun, the Degtyarev, Model 38 is primarily used in anti-aircraft and anti-tank roles.

A notable feature of Soviet armament has been the lack hitherto of any more effective infantry anti-tank weapon than a 14·5-mm anti-tank rifle.

Starting from 1938, there was intensive development of mortars in 50, 82, 107, 120 and 160-mm calibres. In the larger calibres towed mobility on wheeled mountings and carriages and speed into action are the outstanding qualities.

Both anti-personnel and anti-tank (hollow charge) grenades are used.

6. Some of the weapons mentioned on the organization charts are shown in the following pictures.

SECTION 40—SIGNALS

General.

1. A noticeable feature of Soviet Army signals is that more use is made of lines, and less of wireless, than is the case with most other armies.

2. Signal equipment can be placed in three categories:—
  (a) Of pre-war Russian manufacture designed for loose pack and horse transport vehicles.
  (b) Equipment manufactured by other nations, especially British, American and German. The majority of these items are of modern design and were given to the Russians after 1942 in the case of British and American stores, or taken from the Wehrmacht or factories in the case of the German equipment.
  (c) New Russian made equipment largely based on ideas obtained from British, American, and German equipment, and frequently simplified in order to allow for maintenance by indifferent workshop personnel.

There is no evidence to show that any new and original equipment has been produced.

Wireless.

3. Fewer personnel in proportion to the army as a whole are allotted for wireless duties than is the case in the British Army, and the scale

of issue of wireless sets is correspondingly smaller. Armoured and reconnaissance units are better off than infantry units. Within battalions, wireless is little used. The Russians are tending to increase their issue of wireless equipment, but it is clear that an insufficiency of skilled mechanics to maintain the equipment, and skilled operators to work it, do limit the use the Russians can make of wireless for their handling of traffic in the field.

4. There is reason to believe that the Soviet Army is skilled in interception and therefore it should be assumed that it will take full advantage of the signal and cipher security weaknesses of any forces against whom it is operating.

Line.

5. Use is made of lines whenever possible, and line communication systems are often constructed in a remarkably short time by personnel lacking in technical skill, but possessing a great capability for hard work. Teleprinter from army to corps is now standard, and may soon become standard from corps to division.

6. The quality of line stores, especially field cable, is below our own; and, as with wireless, maintenance is a constant difficulty. These two factors make Russian line system less reliable than ours.

Command.

7. Signal officers do not appear to be very skilled, either technically or in the handling of their units. With an imperfect knowledge of what can be done with the men and equipment at their disposal, they tend to promise their staffs communications which cannot be achieved. These weaknesses are known, and efforts to correct them must therefore be expected.

SECTION 41—WEAPONS

7·62-mm Mossin Nagant rifle 91/30

Length without bayonet	— 48½ ins	Magazine capacity	— 5 rds
Weight ,, ,,	— 8·4 lb	Effective range	— 440 yds

Long spike bayonet fits on right side. Sniper's model is fitted with telescopic sight. Latest carbine version is fitted with permanently attached folding bayonet.

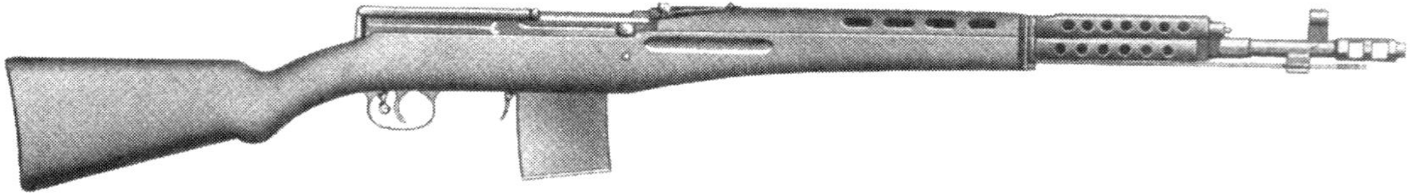

7·62-mm S/L rifle Tokarev, Model, 1940

Length without bayonet	— 48 ins	Magazine capacity	— 10 rds
Weight ,, ,,	— 8½ lb	Effective range	— 440 yds

Blade type bayonet fits below barrel. Sniper's version is fitted with telescopic sight. Gas operated.

7·62-mm machine carbine, Model 1941 "PPSh"

Length overall	— 33 ins	Rate of fire (practical)	—100 rpm
Weight w/o magazine	— 7½ lb	Magazine capacity (drum)	— 71 rds

Single shot or automatic. May also be fitted with box (35 rds) magazine. Flip backsight for 100 and 200 metres, or leaf backsight graduated to 500 metres.

7·62-mm machine carbine, Model 1943 "PPS"

Length overall	— 32½ ins	Rate of fire (practical)	—100 rpm
Weight w/o magazine	— 6 lb	Magazine capacity	— 35 rds

Automatic fire only. Flip backsight for 100 and 200 metres. Butt folds over body.

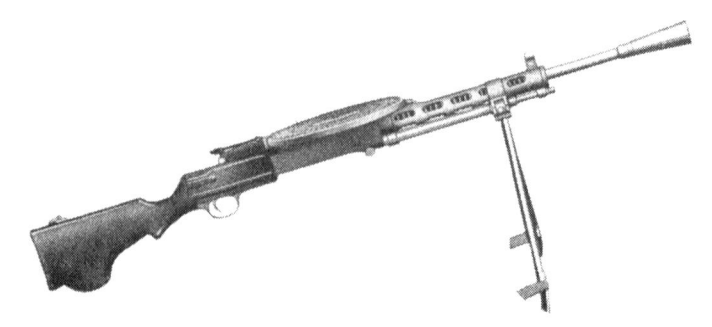

7·62-mm Degtyarev LMG "DP"

Length overall	— 50 ins	Magazine capacity	— 47 rds
Weight w/o magazine	— 18½ lb	Rate of fire (practical)	— 80 rpm

Automatic fire only.

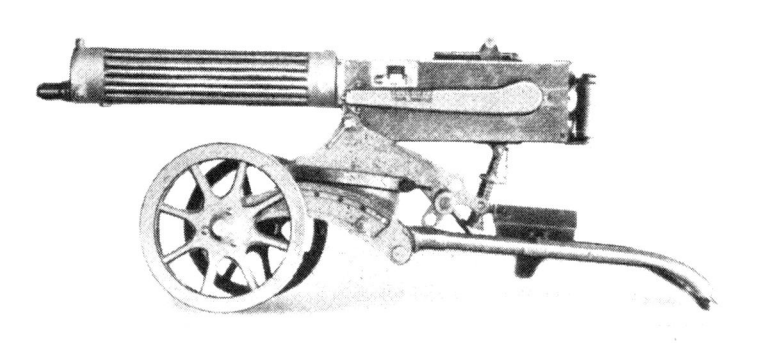

7·62-mm Maxim MMG, Model 1910

Length of gun	— 43 ins	Feed	—250 rd belt
Weight of gun and mounting	— 145 lb	Rate of fire (practical)	—250–300 rpm

12·7-mm Degtyarev HMG, Model 1938

Length of gun	— 64 ins	Feed	—50 rd belt
Weight of gun and mounting	— 397 lb	Rate of fire (practical)	— 125 rpm

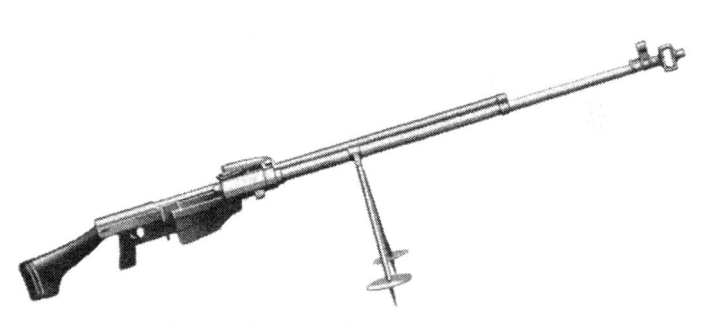

14·5-mm Simonov A tk rifle, Model 1941

Length overall — 84 ins   Feed — 5 rd clip
Weight — 46 lb   Penetration—approx. 30 mm at 110 yds.

Breaks down into two man-loads.

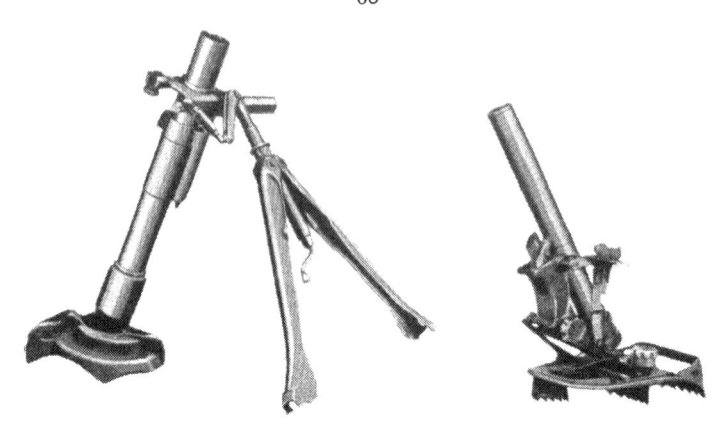

50-mm mortar, Model 1940   **50-mm mortar, Model 1941**

Weight in action	— 20–22 lb	Maximum range	— 875 yds
Weight of bomb	— 2 lb	Maximum rate of fire	— 30 rpm

These mortars are fired at fixed quadrant elevations (45° and 75°). Variations in range are obtained by turning the gas escape control sleeve at the bottom of the barrel.

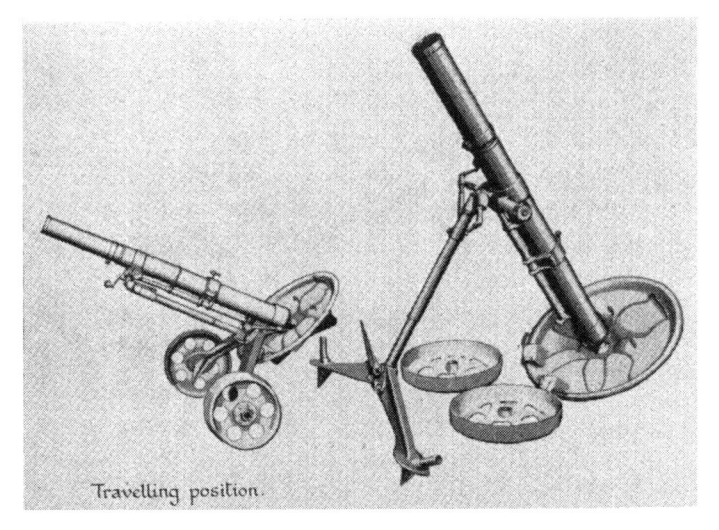

82-mm mortar, Model 1941

Weight on wheels	— 111 lb	Maximum range	— 3400 yds
„ in action	— 100 lb	Minimum range	— 75 yds (approx)
Maximum rate of fire	— 25 rpm	Bomb weight	— 7 lb (approx)

Fires HE, smoke, and illuminating rounds.

On the 1943 model of this mortar the wheels are permanently attached to the bipod.

120-mm mortar, Model 1938

Weight travelling	— 1058 lb	Maximum range	— 6200 yds
,, in action	— 578 lb	Minimum range	— 500 yds
Maximum rate of fire—	12 rpm	Bomb weight	— 35 lb

Optional trigger or gravity fire.

63

13-cm field rocket launcher

A typical Soviet SP field rocket launcher, firing 16 × 13-cm rockets, 8 rockets resting on the guide rails and 8 slung beneath them. Fired electrically from the driver's cab.

4·5-cm A tk gun, Model 42

Weight of shell (AP)	—	1·43 kg	3·151 lb
Maximum range	—	8000 metres	8750 yds
Armour penetration at 300 metres (328 yds)—		95 mm	3.7 ins
Weight in action	—	570 kg	·56 tons

E

5·7-cm A tk gun, Model 43

Weight of shell (AP)	—	3·13 kg	6·9 lb
Maximum range	—	7680 metres	8400 yds
Armour penetration at 300 metres (328 yds)	—	160 mm	6·3 ins
Weight in action	—	1146 kg	1·15 tons

7·62-cm infantry or regimental gun, Model 43

Weight of shell	—	6·2 kg	13·7 lb
Maximum range	—	4200 metres	4600 yds
Armour penetration at 300 metres (328 yds)	—	57 mm	2·3 ins
Weight in action	—	600 kg	11¾ cwts

10·0-cm A tk gun, Model 44

Weight of shell (AP)	— 15·6 kg	34·4 lb
Maximum range	— 21,000 metres	23,000 yds
Armour penetration at 300 metres (328 yds)	— 173 mm	6·8 ins
Weight in action	— 3460 kg	3·4 tons

7·62-cm field/A tk gun, Model 42

Weight of shell	—	6·2 kg	13·7 lb
Maximum range	—	13,000 metres	14,200 yds
Armour penetration at 300 metres (328 yds)	—	110 mm	4·3 ins
Weight in action	—	1116 kg	1·1 tons

12·2-cm field howitzer, Model 38

Weight of shell	—	21·76 kg	48 lb
Maximum range	—	11,800 metres	12,900 yds
Armour penetration at 300 metres (328 yds)	—	100 mm	4 ins
Weight in action	—	2250 kg	2·2 tons

12·2-cm field gun, Model 31/37

Weight of shell	— 25 kg	55 lb
Maximum range	— 20,800 metres	22,750 yds
Armour penetration at 300 metres (328 yds)	— 161 mm	6·3 ins
Weight in action	— 7117 kg	7 tons

15·2-cm medium howitzer, Model 43

Weight of shell	HE —	40 kg	88 lb
	AP —	51 kg	112·3 lb
Maximum range	—	12,460 metres	13,650 yds
Armour penetration at 300 metres (328 yds)—		88 mm	3·46 ins
Weight in action	—	3600 kg	3·55 tons

20·3-cm heavy howitzer, Model 31

Weight of shell	—	100 kg	220·5 lb
Maximum range	—	18,000 metres	19,700 yds
Weight in action	—	17,700 kg	17.4 tons

15·2-cm medium gun howitzer, Model 37

Weight of shell	— 43·5 kg	95·7 lb
Maximum range	— 17,250 metres	18,900 yds
Armour penetration at 300 metres (328 yds)	— 111 mm	4·4 ins
Weight in action	— 7128 kg	7 tons

3·7-cm light anti-aircraft gun, Model 39 Bofors

Weight of shell	— ·73 kg	1·6 lb
Maximum ceiling of burst	— 4000 metres	13,100 ft
Maximum range	— 8000 metres	8750 yds
Armour penetration at 328 yds	— 46 mm	1·8 ins
Weight in action	— 2100 kg	2 tons

8·5-cm heavy anti-aircraft gun, Model 39

Weight of shell	— 9·2 kg	20·2 lb
Maximum ceiling of burst	— 10,500 metres	34,500 ft
Maximum range	— 15,500 metres	17,000 yds
Armour penetration at 300 metres (328 yds)	— 114 mm	4·48 ins
Weight in action	— 4300 kg	4·23 tons

71

T 34-85 medium tank

Weight	— 29 ton 10 cwt.	Crew	— 5.
Armament	— 85-mm (3·3-in) gun.	Armour	— Turret front—100-mm rounded.
	— 2 × 7·62-mm MGs.		— Hull ,, —45-mm at 60°.
Max road speed	— 25 mph		

'Joseph Stalin '3'' heavy tank

Weight—50 tons (approx.).
Armament—122-mm (4·8-in) gun.
—1 × 12·7-mm AA/MG on turret.
Crew—4.
Max road speed 15–16 mph
Armour—
Turret front—200-mm.
—Hull front—120-mm at 55°.

JSU-122

Weight	— 49–54 tons.	Crew	— 5.
Armament	— 122-mm field gun.	Armour	— Mantlet—100-mm rounded.
	— 1 × 12·7-mm AA/MG on roof.		Hull front—100-mm at 70°.
	— 2 × 7·62-mm machine carbines carried loose.		

SU-76

Weight	— 10 tons 16 cwt.	Crew	— 4.
Armament	— 76·2-mm (3-in) gun.	Armour	— Mantlet—15-mm rounded.
	— 2 × 7·62-mm machine carbines carried loose.		— Hull front—25-mm at 60°.

SU-100

Weight	— 30 tons.	Crew	— 4.
Armament	— 100-mm (3·93-in) gun.	Armour	— Mantlet—100-mm rounded.
	— 2 × 7·62-mm machine carbines carried loose.		— Hull front—78-mm at 50°.

JSU-152

Weight	—	50 tons.	
Armament	—	152-mm (6-in) gun.	
	—	1 × 12·7-mm AA/MG on roof.	
	—	2 × 7·62-mm machine carbines carried loose.	
Crew	—	5.	
Armour	—	Mantlet—100-mm rounded.	
	—	Hull front—100-mm at 70°.	

APPENDIX A

HIGH COMMAND
MINISTRY OF THE ARMED FORCES

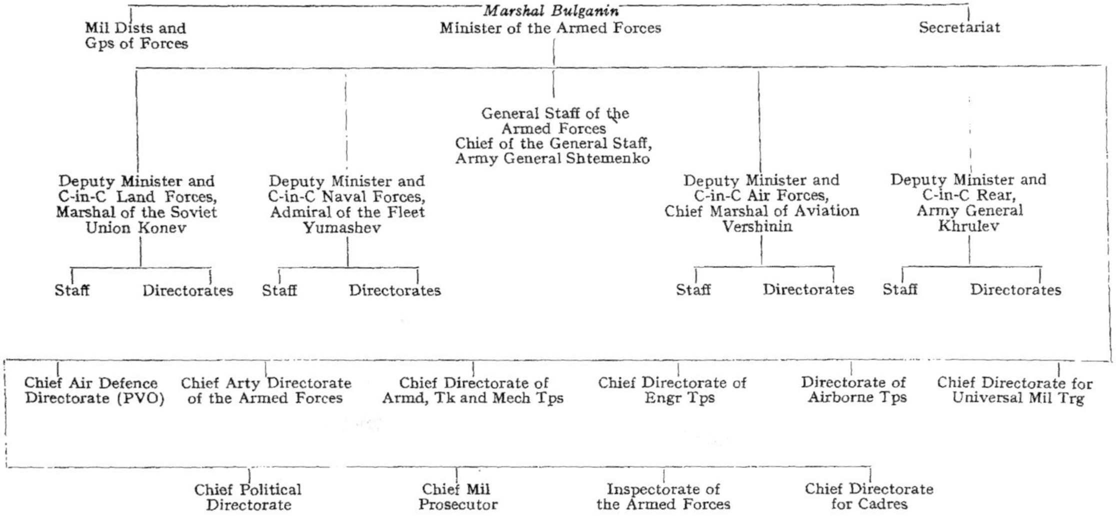

Marshal Bulganin
Minister of the Armed Forces

Secretariat

Mil Dists and Gps of Forces

General Staff of the Armed Forces
Chief of the General Staff, Army General Shtemenko

Deputy Minister and C-in-C Land Forces, Marshal of the Soviet Union Konev
— Staff
— Directorates

Deputy Minister and C-in-C Naval Forces, Admiral of the Fleet Yumashev
— Staff
— Directorates

Deputy Minister and C-in-C Air Forces, Chief Marshal of Aviation Vershinin
— Staff
— Directorates

Deputy Minister and C-in-C Rear, Army General Khrulev
— Staff
— Directorates

Chief Air Defence Directorate (PVO)

Chief Arty Directorate of the Armed Forces

Chief Directorate of Armd, Tk and Mech Tps

Chief Directorate of Engr Tps

Directorate of Airborne Tps

Chief Directorate for Universal Mil Trg

Chief Political Directorate

Chief Mil Prosecutor

Inspectorate of the Armed Forces

Chief Directorate for Cadres

APPENDIX B

A TYPICAL SOVIET FRONT

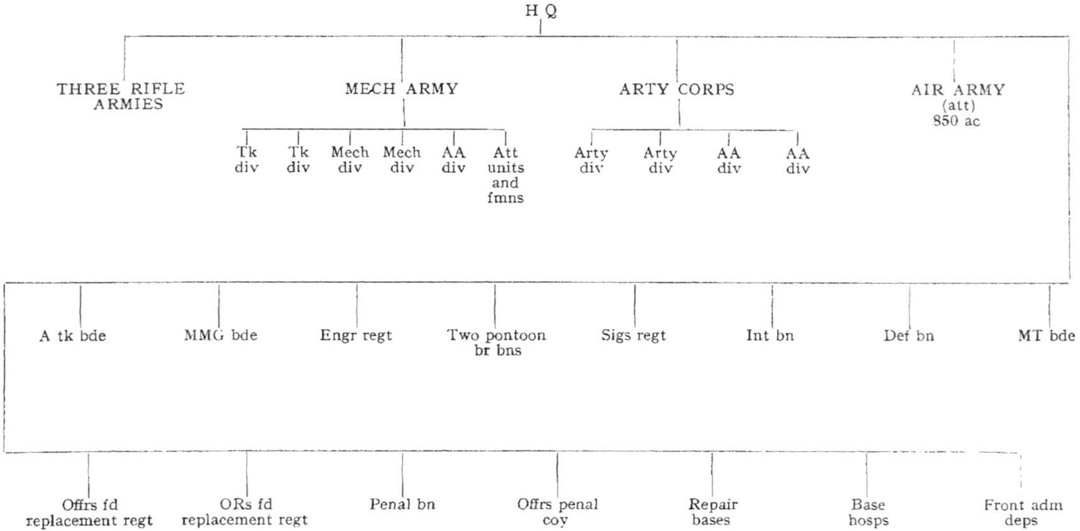

HQ

```
                    ┌──────────────┬──────────────────┬──────────────┐
              THREE RIFLE       MECH ARMY          ARTY CORPS      AIR ARMY
               ARMIES                                               (att)
                                                                   850 ac
                           ┌────┬─────┬─────┬────┬─────┐      ┌─────┬─────┬────┬────┐
                          Tk    Tk   Mech  Mech  AA   Att    Arty  Arty  AA   AA
                          div   div  div   div   div  units  div   div   div  div
                                                      and
                                                      fmns
```

| A tk bde | MMG bde | Engr regt | Two pontoon br bns | Sigs regt | Int bn | Def bn | MT bde |

| Offrs fd replacement regt | ORs fd replacement regt | Penal bn | Offrs penal coy | Repair bases | Base hosps | Front adm deps |

This chart is only a guide to the composition of a typical Soviet front. It should not be taken to imply that all the subordinated formations shown will invariably be found under a front, or that no other formations or units will be allotted. The organization is very elastic, and will vary according to circumstances.

APPENDIX C

A TYPICAL SOVIET RIFLE ARMY
H Q

```
                          ┌─────────────────────┬─────────────────┐
                   THREE RIFLE CORPS      BREAKTHROUGH          AA
                        Each              ARTY DIV              DIV
```

THREE RIFLE CORPS — Each:
Mech div / Rifle div **or** Rifle div — Rifle div — Rifle div — Corps arty bde — AA bty — Sigs bn — Spr regt

Corps arty bde: Gun arty regt (24 × 100-mm guns) — How arty regt (24 × 152-mm hows) — Svy bty

A tk bde: A tk regt 57-mm A tk guns — A tk regt 100-mm A tk guns
 ├─ Bty ─ Tp, Tp, Tp
 └─ Bty
Each 4 × 76.2-mm A tk guns

MMG bde

Engr regt — Bn — Bn (Possibly flame-thrower)

Sigs regt

CW Bn

Balloon observation bty

Def bn — Two int coys

Two MT bns — Wksps bn — Fd replacement Regt (personnel) — Rec depot Rec coy Collecting Coy (captured material) — Army fd PO

Hosps: Fd hosp — Hosp for minor cases — Evac hosp — Vet hosp

Penal bn Penal coy (offrs)

Army clothing dep
Army POL dep
Army amn dep
Army ord deps
Army sups dep

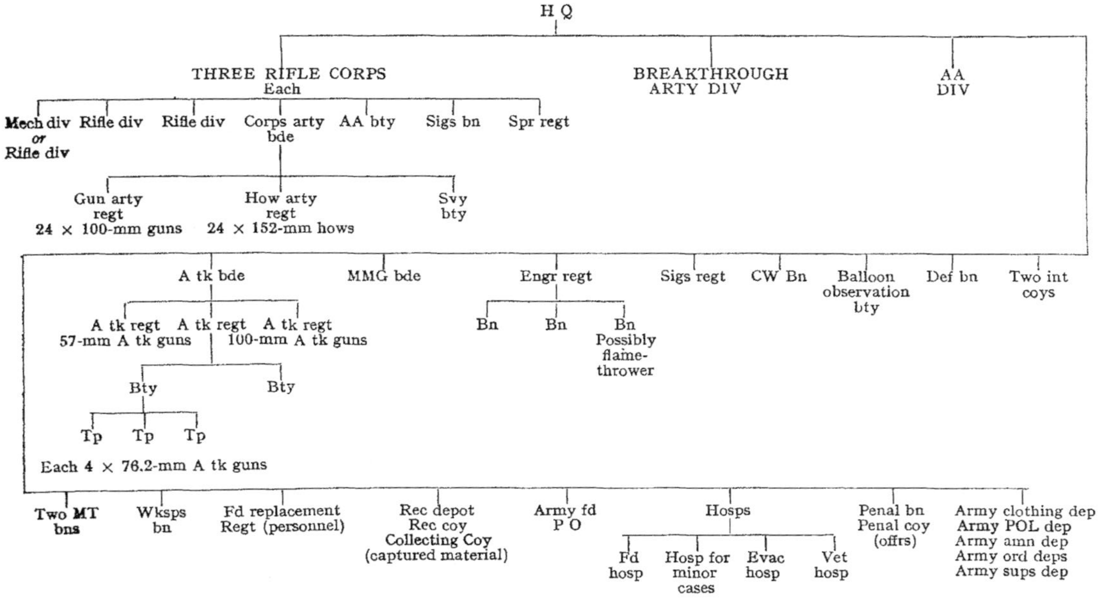

This chart is only a guide to the composition of a typical Soviet rifle army. It should not be taken to imply that all the subordinated formations shown will invariably be found under a rifle army, or that no other formations or units will be allotted. The organization is very elastic, and will vary according to circumstances.

APPENDIX D

80

RIFLE DIVISION (11,013)
Comd and staff gp (250)

THREE RIFLE REGTS

Med tk SP regt (T34/85 tks)
HQ 2 tks
- Tk coy
  - HQ 1 tk
  - Pl — Each 3 × T34/85
- Tk coy
- Tk coy
- SP bty
  - HQ 1 SU100 gp
  - Tp — Each 5 × SU100 guns
  - Tp SP
- Tech and maint gp

Arty[1] Bde
- Comd gp
- Gun arty regt
  - Gun bty — Each 12 × 76.2-mm guns
  - Gun bty
- Svy tp
- Arty maint and sup unit
- Sup pl
- How arty regt
  - How bty — Each 12 × 122-mm hows
  - How bty
- Med pl
  - Mortar bty 12 × 160-mm mortars

MC bn
- MC coy 45 × MC
- MC coy 45 × MC
- Recce coy
  - Pl — Each 4 × MG carriers
  - Pl — Each 6 × 37-mm LAA guns
  - Pl 4 armd C

Spr bn
- Spr coy
- Tech coy incl water sup sec
- Engr pk incl div pontoon pk

Trg bn (att)

Med bn

MT bn and Wksp

HQ coy
- LT Pl
- RT Pl
- Wksp and stores sec
- Msg collecting centre

Sigs bn
- Bty charging sec
- Sup sec
- Tele coy
  - Pl Pl Pl Pl

CW coy

Services
Air liaison flt (3 ac)
Band
Vet sec (a)
Fd bakery
Mil PO

A tk bty
- Tp — Each 4 × 85-mm A tk guns
- Tp

LAA bty
- Tp
- Tp

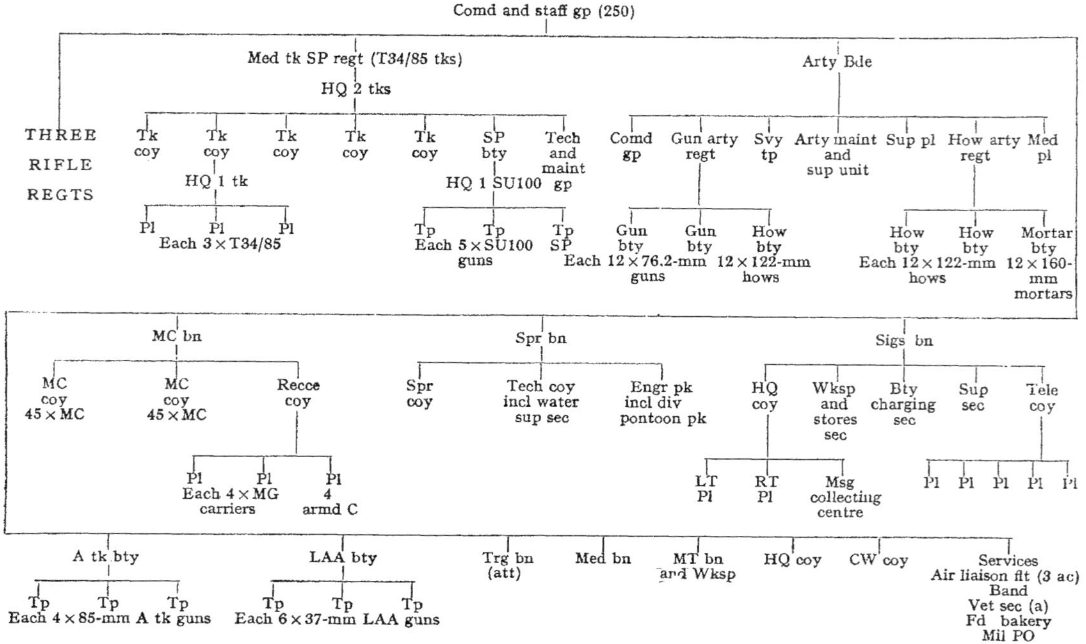

Numbers in brackets refer to personnel strengths.

Note (a). Only included when transport still contains a horse drawn element.

APPENDIX E

RIFLE REGIMENT (2,106)

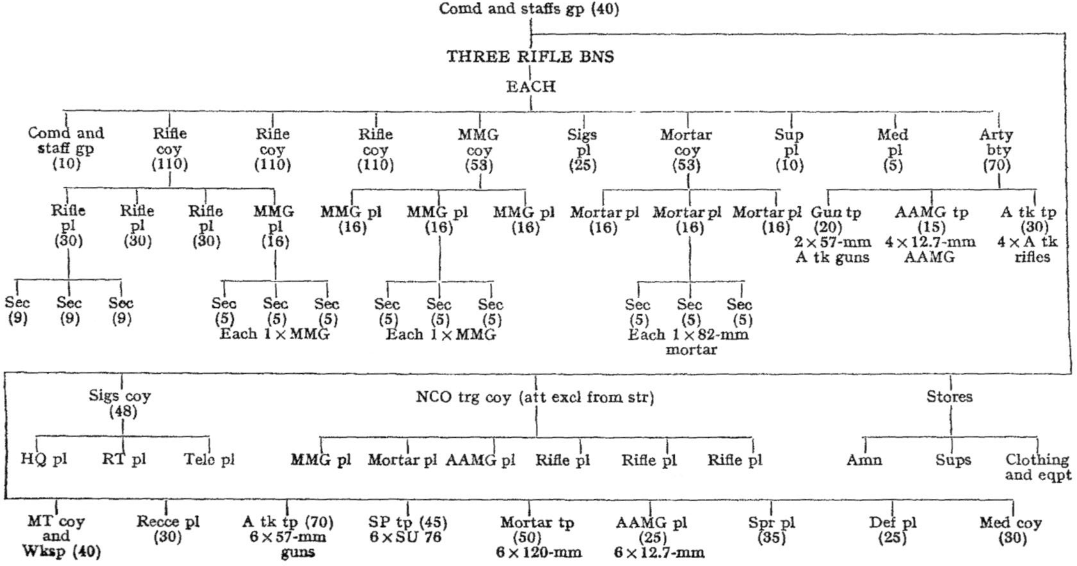

Comd and staffs gp (40)

THREE RIFLE BNS
EACH

- Comd and staff gp (10)
- Rifle coy (110)
  - Rifle pl (30)
    - Sec (9)
    - Sec (9)
    - Sec (9)
  - Rifle pl (30)
  - Rifle pl (30)
  - MMG pl (16)
- Rifle coy (110)
  - MMG pl (16)
    - Sec (5)
    - Sec (5)
    - Sec (5)
    - Each 1 × MMG
- Rifle coy (110)
  - MMG pl (16)
- MMG coy (53)
  - MMG pl (16)
  - MMG pl (16)
  - MMG pl (16)
    - Sec (5)
    - Sec (5)
    - Sec (5)
    - Each 1 × MMG
- Sigs pl (25)
- Mortar coy (53)
  - Mortar pl (16)
  - Mortar pl (16)
  - Mortar pl (16)
    - Sec (5)
    - Sec (5)
    - Sec (5)
    - Each 1 × 82-mm mortar
- Sup pl (10)
- Med pl (5)
- Arty bty (70)
  - Mortar pl (16)
  - Gun tp (20)
    2 × 57-mm A tk guns
  - AAMG tp (15)
    4 × 12.7-mm AAMG
  - A tk tp (30)
    4 × A tk rifles

NCO trg coy (att excl from str)

Sigs coy (48)
- HQ pl
- RT pl
- Telo pl

Recce (30)

- A tk tp (70)
  6 × 57-mm guns
- MMG pl
- SP tp (45)
  6 × SU 76
- Mortar pl
- AAMG pl
- Mortar tp (50)
  6 × 120-mm
- Rifle pl
- AAMG pl (25)
  6 × 12.7-mm
- Rifle pl
- Rifle pl

MT coy and Wksp (40)

Stores
- Amn
- Sups
- Clothing and eqpt

- Spr pl (35)
- Def (25)
- Med coy (30)

Numbers in brackets refer to personnel strengths.

APPENDIX F

MECHANIZED DIVISION (12,844)

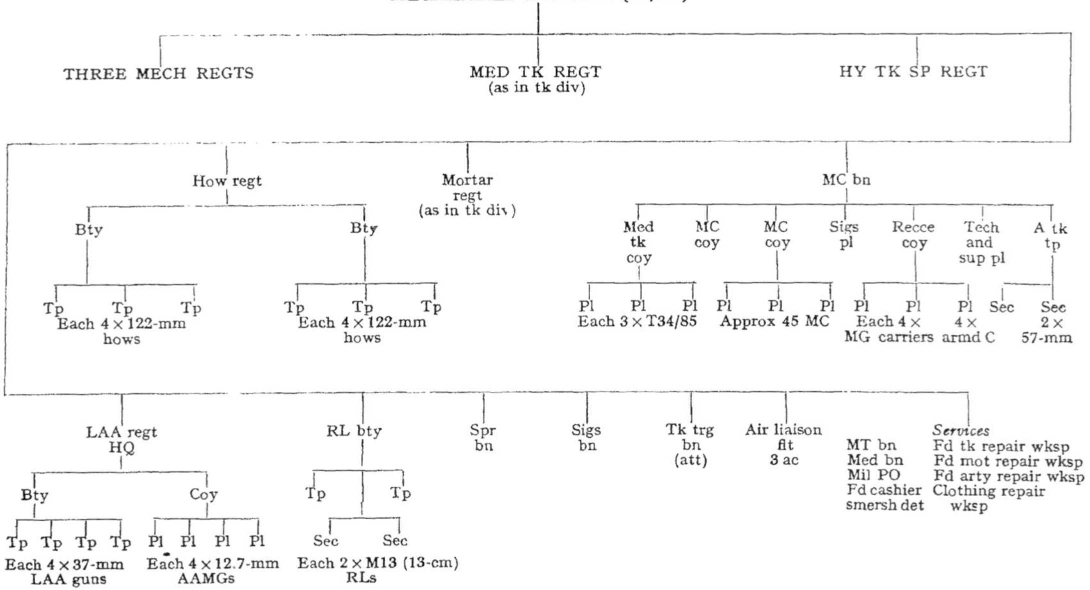

```
                    ┌─────────────────────┬─────────────────────┐
              THREE MECH REGTS      MED TK REGT          HY TK SP REGT
                                    (as in tk div)
```

- THREE MECH REGTS
  - How regt
    - Bty — Tp Tp Tp — Each 4 × 122-mm hows
    - Bty — Tp Tp Tp — Each 4 × 122-mm hows
  - Mortar regt (as in tk div)
  - LAA regt HQ
    - Bty — Tp Tp Tp — Each 4 × 37-mm LAA guns
    - Coy — Pl Pl Pl — Each 4 × 12.7-mm AAMGs
  - RL bty
    - Tp — Sec
    - Tp — Sec
    - Each 2 × M13 (13-cm) RLs

- MED TK REGT (as in tk div)

- HY TK SP REGT
  - MC bn
    - Med tk coy — Pl Pl Pl — Each 3 × T34/85
    - MC coy — Pl Pl Pl — Approx 45 MC
    - MC coy — Pl Pl Pl
    - Sigs pl — Pl
    - Recce coy — Pl Pl — Each 4 × MG carriers armd C
    - Tech and sup pl — Pl — 4 ×
    - A tk tp — Sec — 2 × 57-mm

- Spr bn
- Sigs bn
- Tk trg bn (att)
- Air liaison flt 3 ac
- MT bn
- Med bn
- Mil PO
- Fd cashier smersh det

Services
Fd tk repair wksp
Fd mot repair wksp
Fd arty repair wksp
Clothing repair wksp

Numbers in brackets refer to personnel strengths.

APPENDIX G

MECHANIZED REGIMENT (2,164)

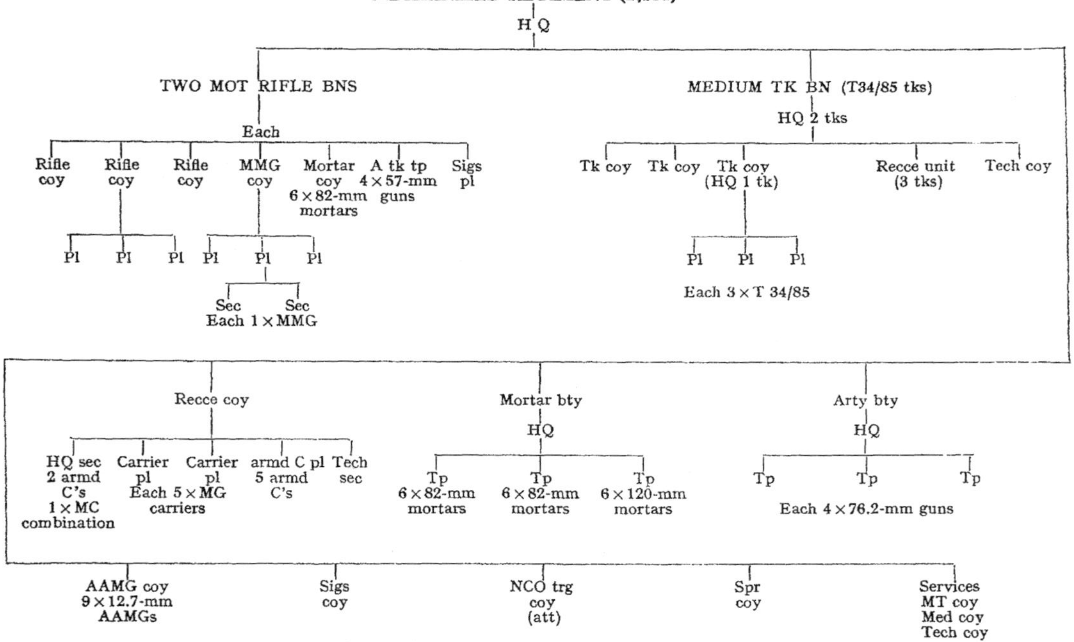

HQ

TWO MOT RIFLE BNS (Each)

- Rifle coy
  - Pl
- Rifle coy
  - Pl, Pl
- Rifle coy
  - Pl, Pl, Pl
- MMG coy
  - Pl, Pl, Pl
  - Sec, Sec — Each 1 × MMG
- Mortar A tk tp coy 4 × 57-mm guns, 6 × 82-mm mortars
- Sigs pl

Recce coy
- HQ sec, 2 armd C's, 1 × MC combination
- Carrier pl — Each 5 × MG carriers
- Carrier armd C pl, 5 armd C's
- Tech sec

AAMG coy 9 × 12.7-mm AAMGs

MEDIUM TK BN (T34/85 tks)

HQ 2 tks

- Tk coy
- Tk coy
- Tk coy (HQ 1 tk)
  - Pl, Pl, Pl — Each 3 × T 34/85
- Recce unit (3 tks)
- Tech coy

Mortar bty
- HQ
- Tp 6 × 82-mm mortars
- Tp 6 × 82-mm mortars
- Tp 6 × 120-mm mortars

Arty bty
- HQ
- Tp, Tp, Tp — Each 4 × 76.2-mm guns

Sigs coy

NCO trg coy (att)

Spr coy

Services
- MT coy
- Med coy
- Tech coy

Numbers in brackets refer to personnel strengths.

APPENDIX H

HEAVY TANK SELF-PROPELLED GUN REGIMENT (1,300)

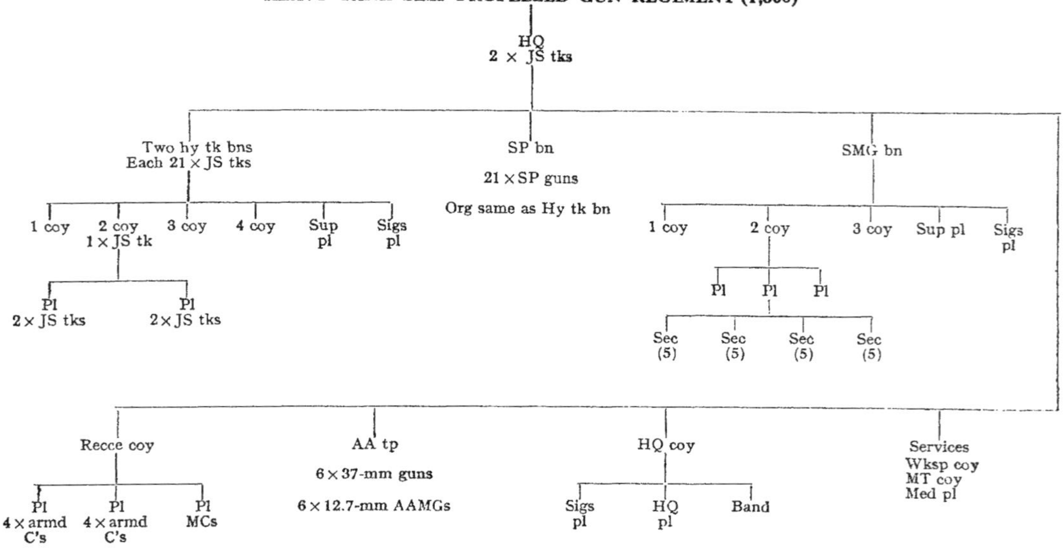

- HQ
  2 × JS tks
  - Two hy tk bns
    Each 21 × JS tks
    - 1 coy
      - Pl
        2 × JS tks
    - 2 coy
      1 × JS tk
      - Pl
        2 × JS tks
    - 3 coy
    - 4 coy
    - Sup pl
    - Sigs pl
  - SP bn
    21 × SP guns
    Org same as Hy tk bn
  - SMG bn
    - 1 coy
    - 2 coy
      - Pl
        - Sec (5)
        - Sec (5)
      - Pl
        - Sec (5)
        - Sec (5)
    - 3 coy
    - Sup pl
    - Sigs pl
  - Recce coy
    - Pl
      4 × armd C's
    - Pl
      4 × armd C's
    - Pl
      MCs
  - AA tp
    6 × 37-mm guns
    6 × 12.7-mm AAMGs
  - HQ coy
    - Sigs pl
    - HQ pl
    - Band
  - Services
    Wksp coy
    MT coy
    Med pl

APPENDIX J

TANK DIVISION (10,659)
HQ + 3 T34/85 tks

- Three med tk regts (T34/85 tks)
  - Each — HQ 1 tk
    - Med tk bn
      - Med tk bn HQ 2 tks
        - Coy Coy Coy HQ 1 tk
          - Pl Pl Pl Each 3 tks
      - Mot rifle bn
        - Coy Coy Coy
        - A tk tp 4 × 57-mm a tk guns
        - Mortar coy 6 × 82-mm mortars
      - AAMG coy 9 × 12.7-mm AAMGs
      - HQ coy
        - Comd pl
        - Recce pl 6 × armd C's
        - Spr pl
        - Sigs pl
        - Med pl
        - Band
      - MT coy

- Mot rifle regt (2155)
  - Rifle bn
    - Coy Coy Coy
    - A tk tp 4 × 57-mm guns
    - Mortar coy 6 × 82-mm mortars
    - Tp 6 × 82-mm mortars
  - Rifle bn
    - Tp 6 × 82-mm mortars
  - Rifle bn
    - Mortar coy 6 × 82-mm mortars
    - Tp 6 × 82-mm mortars
  - Mortar bty
    - Tp 6 × 120-mm mortars
  - AAMG coy 9 × 12.7-mm AAMGs
  - Arty bty
    - Tp Tp Tp Each 4 × 76.2-mm guns

- Hy tk SP regt
- Mortar regt
  - bty
    - Tp Tp Tp Each 6 × 120-mm mortars
  - bty
    - Tp Tp Tp Each 6 × 120-mm mortars
- How bty
- RL bty
  - Tp
    - Sec Sec Each 2 × M 13 (13-cm) RLs
  - Tp
- LAA regt 16 × 37-mm guns 16 × 12.7-mm AAMGs
- Spr bn
- Sigs bn
- MC bn Org same as mech div
- Air liaison flt 3 ac
- Tk trg bn (att)

Services
- MT bn
- Med bn
- Mil PO
- HQ coy
- Fd bakery
- Fd arty repair wksp
- Fd tk repair wksp
- Fd mot repair wksp

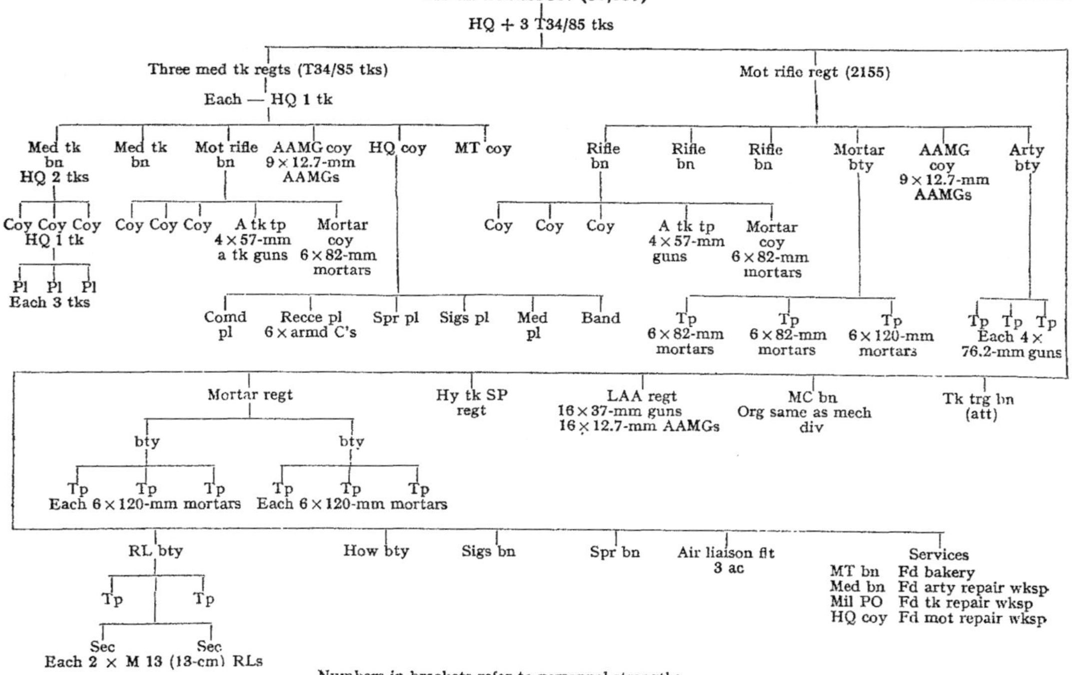

Numbers in brackets refer to personnel strengths

APPENDIX K

'BREAKTHROUGH' ARTILLERY DIVISION (12,000)

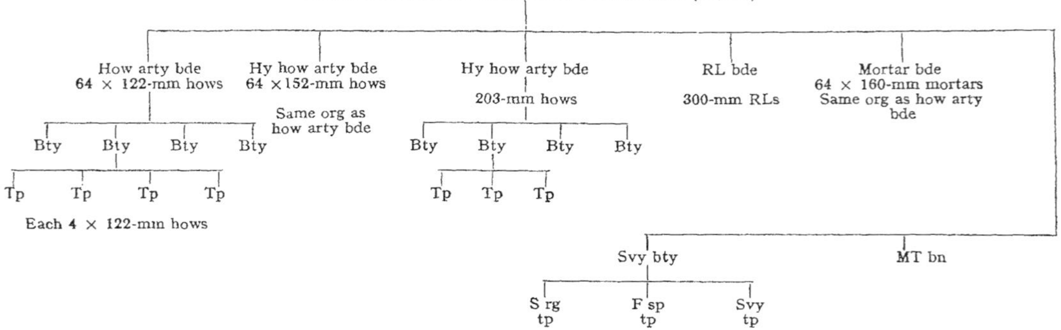

- How arty bde
  64 × 122-mm hows
  - Bty — Tp, Tp, Tp
  - Bty
  - Bty
  Each 4 × 122-mm hows

- Hy how arty bde
  64 × 152-mm hows
  Same org as how arty bde

- Hy how arty bde
  203-mm hows
  - Bty — Tp, Tp, Tp
  - Bty
  - Bty

- RL bde
  300-mm RLs

- Mortar bde
  64 × 160-mm mortars
  Same org as how arty bde

- Svy bty
  - S rg tp
  - F sp tp
  - Svy tp

- MT bn

AA Div (2,380)

- Two LAA regts
  - AAMG coy
    - Pl, Pl, Pl
    Each 4 × 12.7-mm AAMGs
  - Each—
    - Tp, Tp, Tp
    Each 6 × 37-mm LAA guns

- Two HAA regts
  - Each—
    - Tp, Tp, Tp, Tp
    Each 4 × 85-mm HAA guns

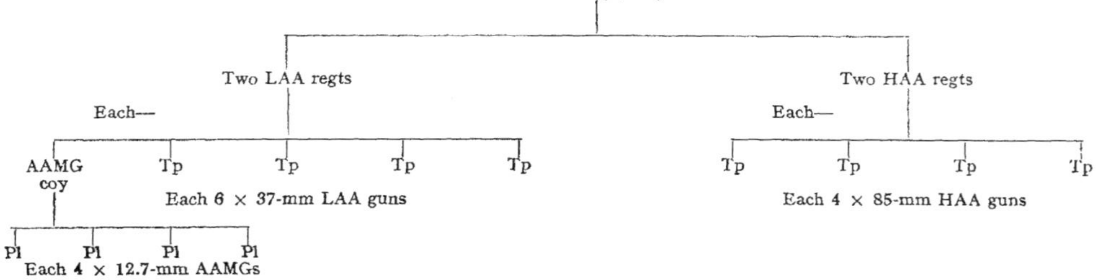

APPENDIX L

PERSONNEL AND EQUIPMENT TABLE FOR A RIFLE DIVISION

UNIT	Personnel	Med tks	Armd Cs	SU 76	SU 100	MCs	Vehs	122-mm hows	160-mm mortars	120-mm mortars	82-mm mortars	57-mm A tk guns	76.2-mm guns	85-mm A tk guns	37-mm LAA guns	12.7-mm AAMGs	MMGs	LMGs	SMGs	Rifles	Pistols	A tk rifles
Three rifle regts	6318	—	—	18	—	18	582	—	—	18	81	36	—	—	54	—	162	279	1146	3789	1383	279
MC bn	450	—	12	—	—	120	21	—	—	—	—	—	—	—	—	—	—	100	225	150	75	—
Med tk/SP regt	700	52	—	—	16	10	80	—	—	—	—	—	—	—	—	—	—	8	150	200	350	—
Comd arty	70	—	—	—	—	3	7	—	—	—	—	—	—	—	—	—	—	—	10	50	10	—
Svy tp	100	—	—	—	—	—	10	—	12	—	—	—	24	—	—	—	—	25	15	75	10	—
Gun arty regt	800	—	—	—	—	15	140	12	—	—	—	—	—	—	—	—	—	25	175	485	140	—
How arty regt	800	—	—	—	—	15	130	24	—	—	—	—	—	—	—	—	—	25	175	485	140	—
Arty maint & sup unit	20	—	—	—	—	—	4	—	—	—	—	—	—	—	—	—	—	—	—	—	2	—
Med pl of arty	5	—	—	—	—	—	1	—	—	—	—	—	—	—	—	—	—	—	—	16	2	—
Sup pl of arty	10	—	—	—	—	—	9	—	—	—	—	—	—	—	—	—	—	—	—	9	1	—
A tk bty	210	—	—	—	—	3	45	—	—	—	—	—	—	12	—	—	—	6	54	102	54	—
LAA bty	250	—	—	—	—	5	45	—	—	—	—	—	—	—	18	—	—	6	70	140	40	—
Spr bn	250	—	—	—	—	5	50	—	—	—	—	—	—	—	—	—	—	14	170	100	50	—
Sigs bn	320	—	—	—	—	—	15	—	—	—	—	—	—	—	—	—	—	—	35	150	35	—
Med bn	220	—	—	—	—	—	10	—	—	—	—	—	—	—	—	—	—	—	—	75	5	—
MT bn & wksps	80	—	—	—	—	—	10	—	—	—	—	—	—	—	—	—	—	—	—	201	26	—
Comd & staff gp	250	—	—	—	—	30	120	—	—	—	—	—	—	—	—	—	—	48	23	67	128	—
Air liaison flt	250	—	—	—	—	—	10	—	—	—	—	—	—	—	—	—	—	—	55	4	8	—
CW coy	10	—	—	—	—	—	1	—	—	—	—	—	—	—	—	—	—	—	3	25	5	—
Band	50	—	—	—	—	—	5	—	—	—	—	—	—	—	—	—	—	—	20	21	5	—
Fd Bakery	30	—	—	—	—	—	3	—	—	—	—	—	—	—	—	—	—	—	4	55	5	—
Mil PO	10	—	—	—	—	—	6	—	—	—	—	—	—	—	—	—	—	—	—	6	4	—
							2															
TOTAL	11013	52	12	18	16	224	1296	36	12	18	81	36	24	12	18	54	—	162	511	2332	6208	2473	279

87

APPENDIX M

PERSONNEL AND EQUIPMENT TABLE FOR A RIFLE REGIMENT

UNIT	Personnel	SU 76	MCs	Vehs	120-mm mortars	82-mm mortars	57-mm A tk guns	12.7-mm AAMGs	MMGs	LMGs	SMGs	Rifles	Pistols	A tk rifles
Recce pl	30	—	—	2	—	—	—	—	—	—	4	22	4	—
Three rifle bns	1668	—	3	120	—	27	6	12	54	90	354	948	366	93
A tk tp	70	—	—	10	—	—	6	—	—	3	18	34	18	—
SP Tp	45	6	2	3	—	—	—	—	—	—	2	3	40	—
Mortar tp	50	—	—	10	6	—	—	—	—	—	—	49	1	—
AAMG pl	25	—	—	7	—	—	—	6	—	—	—	24	1	—
Spr pl	35	—	—	6	—	—	—	—	—	—	—	33	2	—
Def pl	25	—	—	1	—	—	—	—	—	—	3	18	4	—
Sigs coy	48	—	1	7	—	—	—	—	—	—	1	43	4	—
Med coy	30	—	—	4	—	—	—	—	—	—	—	29	1	—
MT coy and wksps	40	—	—	20	—	—	—	—	—	—	—	38	2	—
Comd and staff gp	40	—	—	4	—	—	—	—	—	—	—	22	18	—
TOTAL	2106	6	6	194	6	27	12	18	54	93	382	1263	461	93

APPENDIX N

PERSONNEL AND EQUIPMENT TABLE FOR A RIFLE BATTALION

UNIT	Personnel	MGs	Vehs	82-mm mortars	57-mm A tk guns	12.7-mm AAMGs	MMGs	LMGs	SMGs	Rifles	Pistols	A tk rifles
Three rifle coys	330	—	—	—	—	—	9	27	57	195	78	27
MMG coy	53	—	10	—	—	—	9	—	19	25	9	—
Mortar coy	53	—	10	9	—	—	—	—	19	25	9	—
Arty bty HQ	5	—	1	—	—	—	—	—	1	1	3	—
Gun tp	20	—	2	—	2	—	—	2	6	9	5	—
AAMG tp	15	—	2	—	—	4	—	—	3	9	3	—
A tk rifle tp	30	—	2	—	—	—	—	1	6	20	4	4
Sigs pl	25	—	2	—	—	—	—	—	5	18	2	—
Med pl	5	—	—	—	—	—	—	—	—	3	2	—
Sup pl	10	—	8	—	—	—	—	—	1	8	1	—
Comd staff gp	10	1	3	—	—	—	—	—	1	3	6	—
TOTAL	556	1	40	9	2	4	18	30	118	316	122	31

89

APPENDIX O

PERSONNEL AND EQUIPMENT TABLE FOR A MECHANIZED DIVISION

UNIT	Personnel	Hy tks	Med tks	Armd Cs	Hy sp guns	MCs	Carriers	Vehs	RLs	122-mm hows	120-mm mortars	82-mm mortars	57-mm A tk guns	76.2-mm guns	37-mm LAA guns	12.7-mm AAMGs	MMGs	LMGs	Rifles	SMGs	Pistols
Three mech regts	6492	—	105	21	—	45	30	630	—	—	18	72	24	36	—	27	36	255	3609	1194	1689
Med tk regt	1220	—	65	6	—	21	—	140	—	—	—	6	4	—	—	9	—	30	658	96	466
Hy tk/SP regt	1300	21	—	8	44	21	8	138	—	—	—	—	—	—	—	6	—	30	678	146	476
MC bn	500	—	10	4	—	120	—	22	—	—	—	—	—	—	—	—	—	105	158	218	124
How regt	628	—	—	—	—	15	—	93	—	24	—	—	—	—	16	16	—	25	404	127	97
Mortar regt	508	—	—	—	—	10	—	80	—	—	36	—	—	—	—	—	—	—	354	68	86
LAA regt	316	—	—	—	—	3	—	59	—	—	—	—	—	—	6	—	—	6	252	—	64
RL bty	204	—	—	—	—	2	—	20	—	—	—	—	—	—	—	—	—	8	144	20	40
Spr bn	320	—	—	—	—	5	—	50	8	—	—	—	—	—	—	—	—	14	99	176	45
Air liaison flt	10	—	—	—	—	—	—	1	—	—	—	—	—	—	—	—	—	—	3	4	3
Sigs bn	220	—	—	—	—	—	—	15	—	—	—	—	—	—	—	—	—	—	159	37	24
MT bn	270	—	—	—	—	—	—	180	—	—	—	—	—	—	—	—	—	—	216	22	32
Med bn	80	—	—	—	—	—	—	10	—	—	—	—	—	—	—	—	—	—	75	—	5
Fd tk repair wksp	120	—	—	—	—	—	—	20	—	—	—	—	—	—	—	—	—	—	64	40	16
Fd MT repair wksp	100	—	—	—	—	—	—	10	—	—	—	—	—	—	—	—	—	—	60	30	10
Clothing repair wksp	10	—	—	—	—	—	—	—	—	—	—	—	—	—	—	—	—	—	10	—	—
Fd arty repair wksp	20	—	—	—	—	—	—	10	—	—	—	—	—	—	—	—	—	—	10	5	5
Mil PO	10	—	—	—	—	—	—	2	—	—	—	—	—	—	—	—	—	—	6	—	4
HQ Elements	516	—	3	—	—	52	—	46	—	—	—	—	—	—	—	—	—	48	332	56	128
TOTAL	12844	21	183	39	44	299	38	1521	8	24	54	82	32	36	22	58	36	521	7291	2239	3314

APPENDIX P

PERSONNEL AND EQUIPMENT TABLE FOR A MECHANIZED REGIMENT

UNIT	Personnel	Med tks	Armd Cs	MCs	Carriers	Vehs	120-mm mortars	82-mm mortars	57-mm A tk guns	76.2-mm guns	12.7-mm AAMGs	MMGs	LMGs	SMGs	Rifles	Pistols
Two mot rifle bns	1094	—	—	—	—	94	—	12	8	—	—	12	60	236	614	244
Med tk bn	224	35	—	5	—	5	—	—	—	—	—	—	—	5	60	159
Recce coy	132	—	7	1	10	1	—	—	—	—	—	—	15	64	36	32
Mortar bty	140	—	—	—	—	22	6	12	—	—	—	—	—	17	102	21
Arty bty	226	—	—	3	—	26	—	—	—	12	—	—	6	20	160	46
AAMG coy	36	—	—	—	—	9	—	—	—	—	9	—	—	—	34	2
Sigs coy	48	—	—	1	—	7	—	—	—	—	—	—	—	1	43	4
Spr coy	110	—	—	—	—	7	—	—	—	—	—	—	4	55	39	16
Med coy	30	—	—	—	—	4	—	—	—	—	—	—	—	—	29	1
MT coy and wksps	50	—	—	—	—	25	—	—	—	—	—	—	—	—	47	3
HQ elements	74	—	—	5	—	10	—	—	—	—	—	—	—	—	39	35
TOTAL	2164	35	7	15	10	210	6	24	8	12	9	12	85	398	1203	563

APPENDIX Q

PERSONNEL AND EQUIPMENT TABLE FOR A TANK DIVISION

UNIT	Personnel	Hy tks	Med tks	Armd Cs	Hy SP guns	MCs	Carriers	Vehs	RLs	122-mm hows	120-mm mortars	82-mm mortars	57-mm A tk guns	76.2-mm guns	37-mm LAA guns	12.7-mm AAMGs	MMGs	LMGs	Rifles	SMGs	Pistols
Three med tk regts	3660	—	195	18	—	63	—	420	—	—	—	18	12	—	—	27	—	90	1974	288	1398
Hy tk/SP regt	1300	44	—	8	21	21	8	138	—	—	—	4	4	—	6	6	—	30	678	146	476
MC bn	500	—	10	4	—	120	—	22	—	—	6	30	12	—	—	9	—	105	158	218	124
Mot rifle regt	2155	—	—	—	—	12	—	244	—	—	36	—	—	—	16	16	—	96	1285	390	480
LAA regt	316	—	—	—	—	3	—	59	—	—	—	—	—	—	—	—	—	6	252	—	64
Mortar regt	508	—	—	—	—	10	—	80	—	12	—	—	—	—	—	—	—	—	354	68	86
How bty	350	—	—	—	—	—	—	40	—	—	—	—	—	12	—	—	—	8	270	30	50
RL bty	204	—	—	—	—	2	—	20	12	—	—	—	—	—	—	—	—	8	144	20	40
Sigs bn	220	—	—	—	—	2	—	25	—	—	—	—	—	—	—	—	—	—	159	37	24
Fd arty repairs wksp	20	—	—	—	—	—	—	5	—	—	—	—	—	—	—	—	—	—	10	30	10
Fd tk repairs wksp	120	—	—	—	—	5	—	20	—	—	—	—	—	—	—	—	—	—	64	40	16
Fd MT repairs wksp	100	—	—	—	—	—	—	10	—	—	—	—	—	—	—	—	—	—	60	30	10
Air liaison flt	10	—	—	—	—	—	—	1	—	—	—	—	—	—	—	—	—	—	3	4	3
Spr bn	320	—	—	—	—	—	—	50	—	—	—	—	—	—	—	—	—	14	99	176	45
MT bn	270	—	—	—	—	—	—	180	—	—	—	—	—	—	—	—	—	—	216	22	32
Med bn	80	—	—	—	—	—	—	10	—	—	—	—	—	—	—	—	—	—	40	—	5
HQ elements	516	—	3	—	—	50	—	46	—	—	—	—	—	—	—	—	—	48	342	56	128
Mil PO	10	—	—	—	—	—	—	2	—	—	—	—	—	—	—	—	—	—	4	—	4
TOTAL	10659	44	208	30	21	288	8	1362	12	12	42	52	28	12	22	58	—	405	6139	1530	2990

APPENDIX R

COMPARISON BETWEEN BRITISH AND SOVIET UNITS

Unit or formation	Personnel	Tks	SP guns	Fd guns/bows	Hy mortars	3-in mortars	A tk guns	LAA guns	AAMG	MMG	Vehs	Inf component in personnel
Soviet rifle bn	556	—	—	—	—	9	2	—	4	18	40	556
British inf bn	915	—	—	—	—	6	4	—	—	4	69	915
Soviet rifle div	11013	52	34	60	30	81	36	18	54	162	1296	5619
British inf div	17741	—	—	72	—	54	48 (a)	54	—	36	2928	8455
Soviet tk div	10659	252	21	24	42	52	28	22	58	—	1362	3937
British armd div	17621	290	48	—	—	24	48 (b)	54	—	28	2952	2640
Soviet mech div	12844	204	44	60	54	82	32	22	58	36	1521	5160
Soviet gun arty regt	800	—	—	36	—	—	—	—	—	—	140	—
British fd regt	674	9 (Armd OPs)	—	24	—	—	—	—	—	—	134	—

Notes. (a) Includes 24 SP A tk guns.   (b) All SP A tk guns.

APPENDIX S

HEADQUARTERS OF A RIFLE DIVISION

1. Commander's group.

Divisional commander	Major General
Deputy commander	⎫
Deputy commander for political affairs	⎬ Colonel
Deputy commander for rear services	
Artillery commander	⎭
Staff officer	Captain

2. G Staff.

Chief of staff .. .. .. Colonel

(a) *Ops. group*
Deputy chief of staff	Lieutenant-Colonel
First assistant	Major
Second assistant	Captain

(b) *Intelligence group*
Chief of intelligence	Major
First assistant	Captain or lieutenant

(c) *Signals group*
OC message centre	Senior lieutenant

(d) *Personnel and registration group*
OC group	Major
Personnel officer	Captain
Secret registration officer	Captain

(e) *Cipher Group*
OC Cipher group	Major
First Cipher Officer	Lieutenant
Second Cipher officer	Lieutenant

(f) *Topography*
OC Topography	Captain

3. Political Department.

Assistant deputy commander for political affairs	Lieutenant-Colonel
Head of Komsomol affairs	Major
Deputy head of Komsomol affairs	Captain or lieutenant
Political agitators (2)	Majors
Officer in charge of party organization	Major
Officer in charge of propaganda to local populations	Major or captain

Officer in charge of information
(Editing news) .. .. .. Captain
Secretary of party commission .. Lieutenant-Colonel
or Major
Head of personnel records (Political) Major
Assistant for personnel records
(Political) .. .. Captain or lieutenant

4. Divisional Club.

Head of club .. .. .. Captain
Librarian .. .. Lieutenant

5. Divisional Publications.

Editor .. .. Major
Deputy editor .. .. .. Captain
Writer .. .. Lieutenant

6. Finance.

OC Finance section .. .. Major
Auditor .. .. Captain

7. Artillery section.

Deputy artillery Commander .. Lieutenant-Colonel
Officer in charge of artillery supply Major
Assistant for artillery supply .. Captain

8. Engineer section.

Divisional engineer .. .. .. Major

9. C W section.

Divisional CW officer .. .. Major

10. Q Staff.

(a) *Planning section*
Head of section .. .. .. Major
Assistant .. .. . Captain

(b) *Heads of Services*
Clothing and equipment officer Major
Assistant .. .. .. Captain or lieutenant
Rations and forage officer .. Major
POL supply officer .. .. Major
Assistant .. .. .. Captain or lieutenant
MT officer .. .. .. Major
Medical officer .. .. .. Lieutenant-Colonel
Administration officer .. .. Captain
Assistant .. .. Lieutenant

(c) *Judge advocate's office*
    Judge advocate .. .. .. Major
    Investigating officer .. .. Lieutenant

(d) *Military tribunal*
    President .. .. .. Major
    Secretary .. .. .. Senior Lieutenant

11. Smersh detachment.

3 Majors
1 Captain
2 Lieutenants

APPENDIX T

HEADQUARTERS OF A RIFLE REGIMENT

1. Commander's group.

Regimental commander .. .. Colonel
Deputy commander for political affairs ⎫
Deputy commander for rear services ⎬ Lieutenant-Colonel
Commander of regimental artillery ⎭
Staff officer .. .. Captain

2. G Staff.

Chief of staff .. .. .. Lieutenant-Colonel
Deputy chief of staff .. .. Major

Assistants
Ops. and training.. .. ⎫
Intelligence .. .. ⎬ Captain
Personnel and registration ⎭
PT officer .. .. Lieutenant

3. Political Department.

Officer in charge of party Organization .. .. Major
Head of Komsomol affairs .. .. Senior Lieutenant
Agitator .. .. Major

4. Regimental club.

Head of club .. .. .. Captain
Librarian .. .. Lieutenant

5. Finance.

    Finance officer   ..   ..   ..   **Captain**

6. Q Staff.

Heads of Services
Clothing and equipment officer	
Rations and forage officer	**Captain**
POL supply officer	
MT officer	
Medical officer	**Major or Captain**
Administration officer	**Senior Lieutenant**
Artillery supply officer	**Captain**

7. Smersh detachment.

    Captain
    Lieutenant

HEADQUARTERS OF A RIFLE BATTALION

The headquarter group of a rifle battalion consists of:

    Commander ..   ..   Major
    Deputy commander for political affairs   Captain
    Adjutant   ..   ..   Captain

RESTRICTED

Appendix V

REINFORCED MED TK BN IN DEFENCE

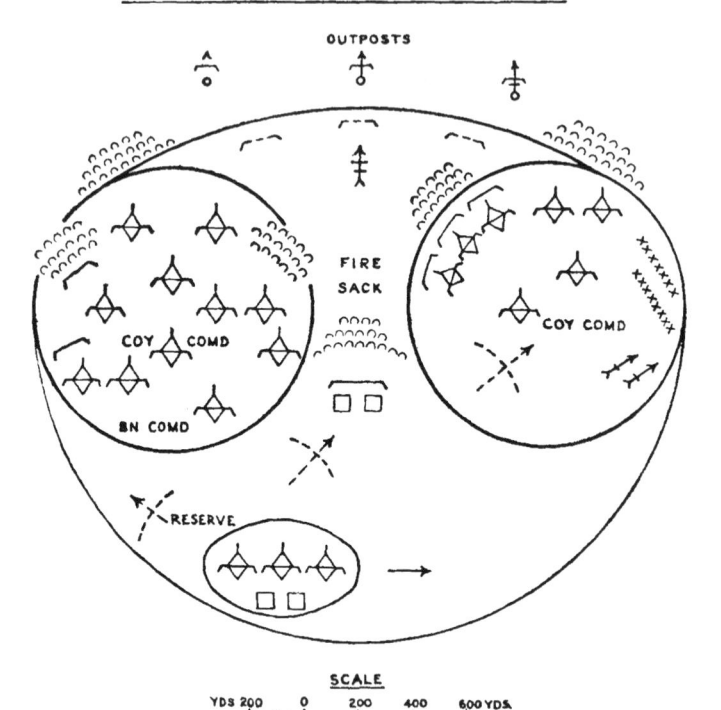

SCALE

YDS 200 0 200 400 600 YDS

REFERENCE

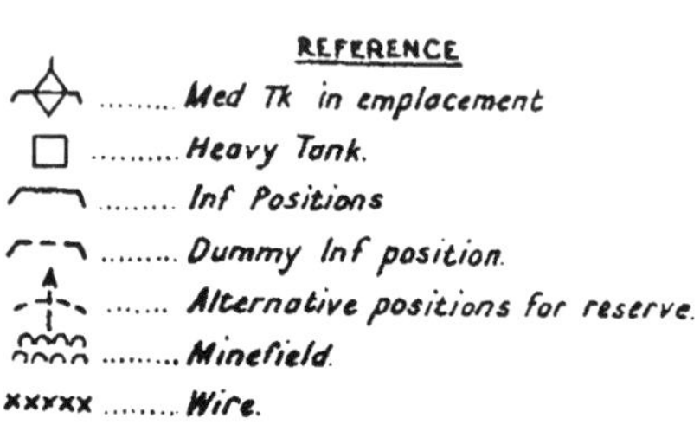

- ⊕ .... Med Tk in emplacement
- □ .... Heavy Tank.
- ⌒ .... Inf Positions
- ⌐ ─ ┐ .... Dummy Inf position.
- ↑ .... Alternative positions for reserve.
- ᴧᴧᴧ .... Minefield.
- xxxxx .... Wire.

Appendix U

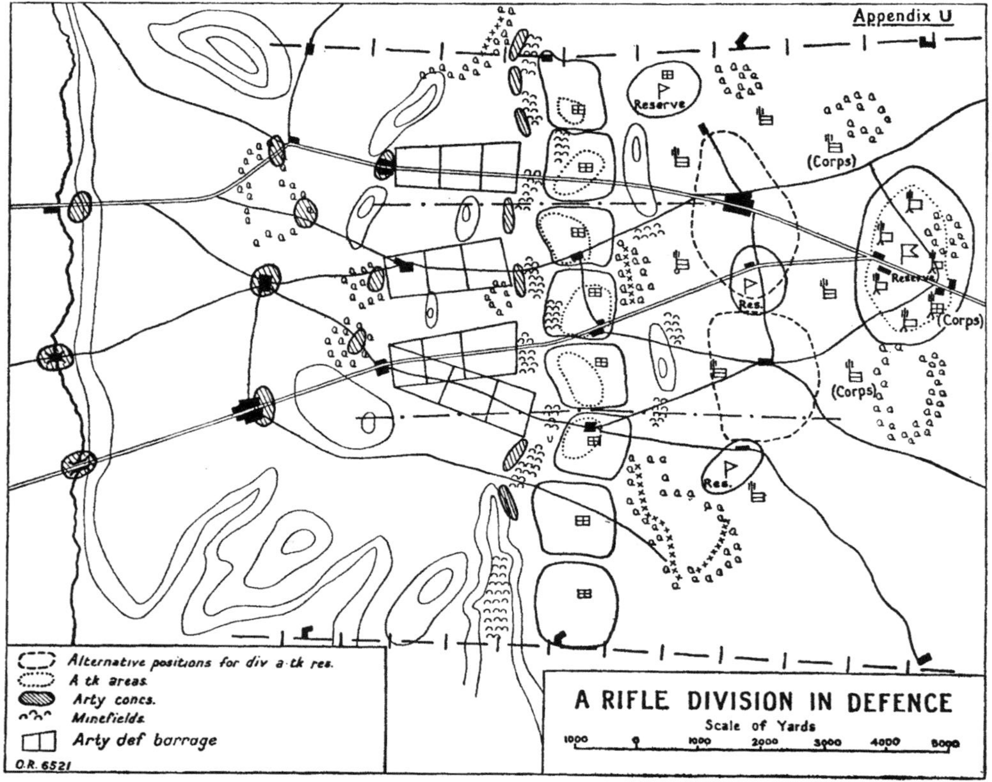

A RIFFLE DIVISION IN DEFENCE

Scale of Yards

Legend:
- Alternative positions for div a tk res.
- A tk areas.
- Arty concs.
- Minefields
- Arty def barrage

O.R. 6521